"*Building Bridges* offers a wealth of information that alone explodes many false notions. But it also takes up the challenge of the hour....It can perform a great service if it becomes a primer book for parents, teachers, pastors, counselors, and those troubled about their sexuality."

William H. Slavick
The Church World

"Homosexuals, their friends and families, and all sensitive Christians have been calling for just this book. It explores the church's stance on homosexuality and examines new approaches to pastoral care and theological evaluations. It is not only for Catholics, but for all who live by the Judeo-Christian value system."

Thomas More Book Club

"*Building Bridges* deserves to become a widely read pastoral classic. Every major authoritative source in the Catholic church, from national bishops to Rome, has called for a sincere and genuine pastoral outreach and presence to gays and lesbians in the church.

"Nugent and Gramick treat their topic with informed knowledge, rich experience, and in a pastorally sensitive way, consonant with Catholic moral teaching. They are sensible in the best sense of embodying and applying rare 'common sense' to a difficult ministry. This book deserves the widest possible readership."

John A. Coleman, S.J.
The Graduate Theological Union

"In this extensive study, the authors treat recent church teaching and controverted positions fair-mindedly, and supply a wealth of evidence to substantiate their case that Roman Catholic approaches have not adequately taken account of the reality of gay experience. Important parts of that reality for Nugent and Gramick are spirituality and the struggle of Catholic gay persons to find a home and make a contribution within their church."

Lisa Sowle Cahill
Boston College

"This book offers a much needed opportunity for further dialogue and understanding concerning gay and lesbian experience and the complex issues that surround this reality. This book not only builds bridges; it breaks new ground for theological reflection, opens new doors for dialogue. Its contents and approach reflect the courage and integrity of its authors."

Sr. Fran Ferder, F.S.P.A., Rev. John Heagle
Co-authors, *Your Sexual Self: Pathway to Authentic Intimacy*

"The wisest voices on the lives of homosexual Christians continue to build bridges. Robert Nugent and Jeannine Gramick give us a clear, careful analysis, laced with practical insights, of the challenges facing both gay and lesbian Christians and the church that professes compassion for them."

James D. Whitehead
Evelyn Eaton Whitehead

"*Building Bridges* is right on target. It is a thorough, sensitive, realistic, and pastorally sound guide for every Catholic lay person, religious, priest, and bishop who is either dedicated to, concerned with, or perplexed and upset by efforts to reach out and build bridges to men and women with gay, lesbian, and bisexual orientations. Nugent and Gramick offer parents, wives, husbands, seminary directors, clerics, and religious superiors solid advice on how to reach out to loved ones struggling to live Christian lives within their 'unconventional' gender orientation."

Robert T. Francoeur, Ph.D.
Fairleigh Dickinson University

"Thank God someone cares—and cares wisely. Our deeply grounded sexual polarities are the scariest and most fascinating levels of the soul. They will be the final taboos and yet the first generators of the spiritual quest. Nugent and Gramick are courageous enough to stay in with their church on this perilous path toward wisdom. I thank them for this book, and I think Jesus does too."

Rev. Richard Rohr, O.F.M.
Center for Action and Contemplation

BUILDING BRIDGES

Gay & Lesbian Reality
and the Catholic Church

Robert Nugent

Jeannine Gramick

TWENTY-THIRD PUBLICATIONS

Mystic, Connecticut 06355

Acknowledgments

The following are acknowledged for their cooperation in allowing us to utilize seminal pieces as a foundation for the chapters in this work: America Press, Inc.; Communications Ministry, Inc.; *Concilium;* Cushwa Center, University of Notre Dame; *Horizon,* National Religious Vocation Conference; *Intellect* and the Society for the Advancement of Education; *Journal of Pastoral Care; Lesbian and Gay Christian Movement Journal;* Quest *Journal;* Robert T. Francoeur, Ph.D.; *The Tablet* (London).

Third printing 1995

Twenty-Third Publications
185 Willow Street
P.O. Box 180
Mystic CT 06355
(203) 536-2611
800-321-0411

ISBN 0-89622-503-8
Library of Congress Catalog Card Number 91-67051
Printed in the U.S.A.

Foreword

Controversies involving new and significantly different kinds of human behavior have frequently arisen in the last few years in our society. Homosexuality is one such issue. The Roman Catholic church like society in general is grappling with how to respond to the gay and lesbian reality. In the midst of such turmoil, strident voices, bitter denunciations, and angry epithets often fill the air.

Jeannine Gramick and Robert Nugent in *Building Bridges: Gay & Lesbian Reality and the Catholic Church* avoid the temptation of name-calling and angry recriminations. The book calmly and clearly explains how the authors envision the Roman Catholic church's approaches to gays and lesbians in the midst of the present controversy. I was impressed by the love of the church, deep concern for people, and in-depth knowledge of the subject matter which are evident throughout this volume. The book truly lives up to its title—*Building Bridges*—between the Roman Catholic church and the gay and lesbian reality.

Jeannine Gramick and Robert Nugent are very well equipped for their task. They have been working in ministry with gay and lesbian Catholics for two decades. Gramick and Nugent have lectured widely in this country and abroad. There are probably no others who have more contacts with the Catholic lesbian and gay community. This book is the fruit of their study, experience, and ministry of the last twenty years.

Building Bridges can also serve as a very handy resource for all aspects of the relationship between the church and the lesbian and gay reality. Catholic gays and lesbians will find the book very helpful. Above all, the parents of gays and lesbians will find these pages most helpful. I was surprised recently to hear from the faculty adviser to the gay and lesbian group at a prominent American institution of higher learning that thirty percent of the gays were troubled by the fact that they had not communicated with their parents about their sexuality.

All those involved in ministry in the Catholic church can profit immensely from reading this book. The authors touch all the important issues: the explanation of the development of our sexuality, the human and political rights of lesbians and gays, the myths that so often arise in these areas, the life of the lesbian and gay person in religious communities and in the priesthood. One-fourth of the book deals with evolving theological perspectives in the Roman Catholic church.

The authors have carefully articulated some contemporary developments and alternative approaches within the Catholic community to the ethical and pastoral questions about homosexuality and the experiences of gay and lesbian Catholics. Not all readers, myself included, will find themselves in full agreement with some of the proposals being offered in the theological community. However, all must admire the ability and willingness of Jeannine Gramick and Robert Nugent to acquaint their readers with what is being said and done today. I respect their careful reasoning, the pastoral insights resulting from their own experience, and the irenic tone and approach found throughout the whole book.

Building Bridges furnishes an excellent concrete example of how to deal with controversial issues in the church. We are all familiar with the turmoil that has existed in the Roman Catholic church in the last twenty-five years. Many Catholics look upon these years as an aberrant and exceptional experience while they yearn for the peace and quiet of the pre-Vatican II church. Such a romantic nostalgia for the lack of controversy within the church is itself based on an illusion.

The pages of church history refute the simplistic understanding of a totally peaceful and tranquil church life. Think of the controversies in the fourth, fifth, and subsequent centuries about the very meaning of our faith in the Trinity and in Jesus Christ. Only at that time did the church work out in the midst of controversy its understanding of the Trinity as involving three persons and one nature whereas in Jesus there are two natures and one person.

The Catholic church has often known controversy and tension in its attempt to understand and practice the moral life of the community of the disciples of Jesus. Contemporary Catholics are well aware of the controversy, for example, over artificial contraception in the light of the papal encyclical *Humanae Vitae* which condemned artificial contraception for Catholic spouses in 1968.

However, controversy over moral questions is not something new in the church. Saint Alphonsus Liguori (d. 1789) has been declared a saint and the patron of Catholic moral theology, but his life was involved in many controversies. The seventeenth and eighteenth centuries in Catholicism witnessed the fierce struggle in moral theology and in the moral life between groups that often characterized one another as rigorists and laxists. Alphonsus was often caught in the middle between these two groups and frequently labeled a laxist. The future saint was the victim of a strong attack by a pseudonymous author. The church censors in Naples were unwilling to grant him permission to publish some of his works in Naples. Alphonsus tells of going out in a boat into the bay of Naples to rendezvous with a ship coming from Venice bringing copies of his book so that he could smuggle them into Naples. Alphonsus thus reminds us that the life of a moral theologian is never simple!

Controversy and tension will always be a part of the life of the

church. Without tension the church itself is dead. The Catholic
church, to its great credit, has always emphasized the need for
creative fidelity to the word and work of Jesus. Unlike some of a
more fundamentalist persuasion, the Catholic church has never
said that the church merely repeats again and again the word of
the Scriptures. Rather the Scriptures must be understood,
proclaimed, appropriated, and lived in the light of the ongoing
historical and cultural circumstances of time and space. The
Christological and Trinitarian controversies of the early church
remind us that the church can find even in secular sources the
wisdom that helps it to understand and express better the myster-
ies of faith. However, history also reminds us of those who have
abandoned the tradition in the light of the purported claims of
modernity or of the alleged needs of the present moment. Creative fidelity well expresses the reality that the church strives for.
In the midst of controversies and disputes over particular issues
one never knows for sure what creative fidelity calls for. In these
situations all concerned must strive to avoid unnecessarily exacer-
bating the tensions that will always be a part of the life of the pilgrim church.

   In the light of this context the contribution of Jeannine Gramick
and Robert Nugent is all the more significant. Not only have they
provided an approach to homosexuality that is compassionate
and truly catholic (all-embracing), but they have also modeled
how people in the church should deal with the controversial issues that will always be a part of our life. In its content and in its
approach *Building Bridges* well exemplifies the creative fidelity
and catholic respect for all concerned that should characterize the
life of the pilgrim church as it strives to do the truth in love.

Charles E. Curran
Elizabeth Scurlock Professor of Human Values
Southern Methodist University

Preface

For more than twenty years we have engaged in what we have called a bridge ministry of justice and reconciliation for gay and lesbian Catholics and the larger church community. In these years we have witnessed a colorful mixture of complex events and personalities which have intersected with each other and influenced us. They have been interesting and, at times, exciting years. They have brought us diversified and rich experiences of human and church reality, though not always without personal pain and suffering.

When we have been tempted to be discouraged and angry, the support of co-workers and friends, both in the United States and abroad, has sustained our energies, our vision, and our hopes. This has been more than sufficient reward for the personal and political stresses which have characterized our efforts for education, pastoral care, and the fundamental dignity of those with whom and for whom we minister. We remain hopeful that the personal changes and steady institutional growth we have witnessed over the years in positive attitudes and practices toward gay and lesbian people will continue as the church wrestles with theological and pastoral issues.

We are especially grateful to Charles Curran for his foreword to this book. We first met Charlie in Washington in the late 1970s when he was in the midst of his own, not then public, "dialogue" with the Vatican. Charlie was a major speaker at the first New Ways Ministry symposium where he was publicly challenged by Brian McNaught for his mediating position on homosexuality, which Brian found too traditional! We discovered in Charles Curran a priest who always had time to offer sound theological advice, inspire personal courage, and share the healing balm of laughter and humor with anyone who approached him. We have experienced his well-known, gentle ability to offer spiritual and physical hospitality. We cherish fond memories of late night strategy sessions with him in his Caldwell Hall suite where we went seeking advice on how to respond to growing Vatican pressures. Charlie has been for us, and for thousands of others, one of the finest exponents of an authentic and healthy Catholic moral tradition. He shows us an unwavering fidelity to the church's commitment to stand in the truth with courage and integrity. We have even had the honor to have been among the first to sample his apartment cuisine on a visit to Auburn in 1990 during a seminar tour of the deep South!

We hope that the experiences and analyses presented here will reach a wide audience. Over the years it has often been suggested that we gather some of our writings in one place because most people do not necessarily have access to specialized journals. From our previously published articles, we have selected those which address four specific themes: educational and social concerns, counseling and pastoral issues, religious and clerical life, and evolving theological perspectives. All of these articles have been substantially revised to incorporate and reflect evolving church positions, current scientific research, and contemporary theological developments in the field. They are complemented by some chapters that have never appeared in print before in any form.

We want to thank Mike Bushek for the many hours he devoted to the typing of drafts and rewrites of the chapters, and for his patience with temperamental computers. We are also grateful to Kurt Schade, Brad Milunski, for their helpful proofreading and editorial suggestions. Special thanks go to Brad for his invaluable aid in compiling the index.

We offer these essays with a modest hope that they will encourage readers to make their own unique contributions to this ministry in which all of us are engaged in one way or another. We all know lesbian and gay people. They are among the finest ministers in the church on every level. We grieve with those who are tempted to abandon the institutional church because of its reluctance to engage in an honest dialogue with gay and lesbian Catholics and its harsh or even unconscious insensitivity to the reality of their lives and faith. We understand the pain which impels many to seek spiritual nourishment elsewhere. We make no excuses for the bigotry and hostility unfortunately manifested by some who call themselves followers of Christ. We salute the brave lives of thousands of gay and lesbian Catholics over the years who have chosen to claim their Catholic identity, refused to allow anyone to exclude them from their rightful heritage and tradition, and now offer their experiences of being Catholic and lesbian or gay to the wider church for reflection and response.

It is to all these gay and lesbian Catholics, to those who minister with and to them, to their families and friends, and to all those in the church who value this ministry and who are willing to support its continuation that we pledge our ongoing efforts to the constructive project of building bridges in the coming years.

Dedication

We dedicate this book to the present and past leadership of the School Sisters of Notre Dame and the Society of the Divine Savior. These individuals themselves have shared at times in the difficulties we have encountered in this ministry. They have not only encouraged and supported us, but also worked hard at trying to personally understand our work. They have also challenged us along the way and called us to accountability. We especially want to recognize the courage and vision of the following SSND U.S. Provincials: Francis Regis Carton, Ruth Marie May, Patricia Flynn, and Christine Mulcahy; and that of the following SDS U.S. Provincials: Myron Wagner, Justin Pierce, Barry Griffin, and Paul Portland. Our Generalate leaders in Rome have also played major parts at some very crucial times in our history: Mother Georgianne Segner, Mary Margaret Johanning, Patricia Flynn, Gerard Rogowski, and Malachy McBride. Finally, we want to recognize all those "collegial" bishops who, in small and large gestures, both in public and in private, have indicated their support, gratitude, and encouragement for what we are doing. The style of leadership of all these people, their unwavering commitment to justice, and their personal comfort with their own humanity and that of others have been for us both strength and hope.

Contents

"It was then—so late in life!—I began to understand what the people need from us, their pastors, and what I, who am the Shepherd over all, had so rigidly denied them. They do not need more laws, more prohibitions, more caveats. They act most normally and most morally by the reasons of the heart. They are already imprinted with the graffito of God. They need a climate of love and compassion and understanding in which they can grow to their full promise—which, my dear brothers, is the true meaning of salvation."

Pope Leo XIV's Address to the College of Cardinals
—from Morris West's *Lazarus*

BUILDING BRIDGES

–1–

Gay and Lesbian Rights

In 1969, in the city of New York, history was made on a hot Friday night in June when the city police routinely attempted to raid a popular bar on Christopher Street which was a meeting place for homosexual men and transvestites. The bar was located in Greenwich Village, for decades a haven for poets, beatniks, hippies, artists, writers, and dozens of other kinds of people whom society often pushes to the fringes. Its name, the Stonewall Inn, is now synonymous with one of the turning points of the modern gay and lesbian liberation movement in the United States.

At the "Stonewall Rebellion" the patrons of the bar decided, spontaneously it seems, to resist the traditionally accepted harassment of the police. Resistance from the "sissies" and the "queers" caught the police unprepared. At one point the police found themselves locked inside the bar and the patrons outside throwing bottles and calling names. Reinforcements were called in and the crowds were dispersed. On the following night, however, a large crowd of gay men and their supporters gathered in Sheridan Square to protest the police action. When the police arrived, another confrontation took place and continued for several days. Eventually things returned to normal. But for the people who experienced that event, and for the thousands of homosexual men and women ever since, the "normal" life of pretending, hiding, and denying would never be the same again.

The gay liberation movement came to prominence in 1969. It is commemorated each June with the Christopher Street Parade in New York and marches, cultural events, and celebrations of gay and lesbian pride in almost every major U.S. city and even in smaller towns throughout the U.S. Before 1969, however, separate organizations of lesbians and gay men both on the East and West coasts, like the Mattachine Society and the Daughters of Bilitis, were already attempting to obtain fairer treatment from society. Timid at first, these early pioneers, through their educational projects and support groups, helped break ground for later political and social gains that gay and lesbian citizens enjoy today.

Religion, Law, and Medicine

Gay and lesbian people have had to contend with three major institutions in our society that shape and mold our thinking and feelings about homosexuality. Since the Stonewall Rebellion major changes have taken place in medicine, religion, and law. Although these institutions still evidence great ambiguity about homosexuality, all of them have modified their former judgments to some extent.

The majority of psychiatrists and psychologists, although not all, do not believe that being gay or lesbian is a form of mental illness or emotional disturbance. Some major Christian and Jewish denominations include reputable theologians who do not believe that all homosexual behavior is immoral. By 1991 only 25 states and the District of Columbia still considered sodomy a felony or a misdemeanor. Other states either repealed the law or had no such law on the books. Although sodomy is generally understood to mean anal intercourse between two males, historically and legally it has also included anal and oral sex between a husband and wife and forms of sexual behavior that are other than heterosexual, genital intercourse. When discussing homosexuality we need to avoid the error of equating sodomy with homosexual behavior. There are gay men who do not engage in anal intercourse. Nor should we assume that heterosexual people cannot also engage in sodomy less strictly defined.

Civil Rights

The gay and lesbian liberation movement has concentrated on securing for gay and lesbian people the same kinds of legal rights that are enjoyed by other minorities in our society. One approach has been to obtain legal protection against arbitrary discrimination in critical areas such as employment, housing, and public accommodations. In the media this struggle is usually called the gay rights movement. Legislation on both federal and state levels is called gay rights laws.

There is a common misunderstanding, whether deliberate or accidental, that homosexual people are asking for special consideration or special laws that other groups or individuals in our country do not enjoy. This is not true. Gay and lesbian people involved in the campaign for their civil rights are asking for the same protection and guarantees that African Americans, women, Hispanics, and others have sought. They see themselves as members of a minority group just as African Americans and women often do because gay and lesbian people compose only ten percent of our society. Being numerically a minority does not necessarily imply social discrimination; left-handed people and redheads are minorities who do not experience discrimination. But when the majority characteristic, such as whiteness, maleness, or heterosexuality, is judged superior or considered the norm for full acceptance or equality, then the minority status does evoke discrimination.

Some people find the analogy between race and homosexuality difficult to understand. They acknowledge the injustice of discrimination against African Americans and women because, generally speaking, people do not choose their race or gender. The hidden assumption in this objection to gay rights is that lesbian and gay people choose their homosexuality. It is important not to confuse homosexual orientation, where there is no choice, with homosexual behavior, where there is personal choice. A homosexual orientation means that a particular individual is attracted predominantly to some individuals of the same gender. The attraction is not only an erotic, physical attraction, but even more importantly, an inner, emotional, or romantic attraction. A true homosexual orientation has more to do with the gender of the person one falls in love with than the gender of the person one has sex with. Some sexual educators are creating new categories by defining sexual or erotic orientation as only one facet of gender orientation (Francoeur, 1991).

People who understand why society ought not to discriminate against people because of race or gender can often understand why citizens should not suffer discrimination because of their sexual orientation. Likewise those who oppose rights for lesbian and gay people often use the same arguments and tactics against homosexual people as were and are still used against women and African Americans. These minorities were required by criminal law to keep within limited boundaries of "acceptable" behavior.

An extreme form of this kind of discrimination can be found in South Africa's apartheid system, which instituted policies to keep certain groups physically limited by imposing geographical boundaries affecting place of residence.

There are strong analogies between the movement for racial equality and the movement for equality for gay and lesbian people, although there are also some striking differences. Before considering particular areas of discrimination against homosexual people that can and ought to be eliminated by sound legislation, it will be important to anticipate one objection particularly that is commonly heard from those groups and individuals who oppose gay rights.

Common Objections

Homosexual people have often been called the invisible minority. Despite the popular belief that "you can always tell homosexuals" by their walk, dress, or occupation, the vast majority of lesbian women and gay men remain hidden from society at large and, many times, from their own families and friends. With the advent of the Stonewall Rebellion and the gay and lesbian liberation movement, more and more homosexual people are publicly identifying themselves as gay or lesbian. But pressures are still strong to make them remain hidden. Those who object to gay rights legislation contend that the only time homosexual people suffer from discrimination or persecution is when they identify themselves as such. "If no one knew they were homosexual, they would have no problems."

This essentially says that in order to be treated fairly and justly a gay or lesbian person must constantly deny or hide a part of his or her humanity that is central to living a full, human life. It is comparable to telling African Americans or Jewish people that the only way they can be treated equally is for them to pass as white people or as Gentiles, and to deny their racial identity. Some light-skinned African Americans have attempted to do this in order to fit into U.S. society. In Nazi Germany some Jewish people did the same in order to escape the death camps. The cost of such denial, however, to one's sense of integrity and self-worth cannot be measured.

Up to this point it has been argued that individuals ought not to suffer discrimination in our society because of something over which they have no choice, such as race, gender, or sexual orientation, and which is important to them as they live out their human lives. People of good will can see the logic of this approach. When it comes to lesbian and gay people, however, there are other considerations that enter into the thinking of those opposed to laws protecting homosexual people against discrimination in employment, housing, and other areas.

The objection that is often heard against gay rights laws, especially as they apply to certain jobs, is that such legislation could be seen as condoning, justifying, or approving homosexual behavior or a lifestyle that many people oppose on religious grounds. Same-sex behavior, for some people, is "against nature," "immoral," or "condemned by the Bible." These people are concerned that legal approval or protection of gay and lesbian persons will also imply societal approval of homosexual expressions. According to this position, homosexual behavior is harmful to society, and we ought not to give it any kind of approval.

If our laws embody certain moral beliefs and principles, then they also teach people what is right and wrong. Society, it is said, has a stake in heterosexuality and family life and ought to promote these values whenever possible. Laws protecting homosexual people in jobs and housing will send signals to young people that homosexuality is perfectly all right. This is something we ought not to do, they believe.

While this position merits serious consideration and rational dialogue in a pluralistic society that claims a Judeo-Christian basis and value system, it is also marred with serious flaws which need to be pointed out. First of all, the laws that protect gay and lesbian people in jobs and guarantee them protection against discrimination in housing are clearly written to protect a person's sexual orientation if it becomes a matter of public knowledge. These laws have nothing to do with sexual behavior, which is a private matter.

A comparison might be made with laws guaranteeing freedom of religion. The state can take a neutral stance toward particular religions while protecting and promoting freedom of religious belief and practice. The only time the state cannot maintain neutrality is when the practice of a certain religion would cause serious harm to individuals or the public order. The state might want to intervene, for example, if a particular religion prohibits medical care. It has done so in the case of parents who were Christian Scientists who refused to provide medical treatment for their child because of their religion.

Can the state, while promoting the value of human sexual identity through the enactment of legislation that protects heterosexual, bisexual, and homosexual orientation of individuals, maintain a neutrality concerning the concrete expressions of these orientations in so far as they do not harm the common good? This is not to deny the right and responsibility of religious groups to promote certain values and concepts of sexuality, marriage, and family life in society. But it does assert that others might come to different conclusions about sexuality. Even the traditional definitions of marriage and family are being tested in the marketplace of a free and pluralistic society. It is rather unlikely that homosexuality will ever replace the heterosexual mode of human sexuality. Given the historical predominance of the heterosexual lifestyle and its strong support in laws, culture, and religion, it is surprising to hear the opponents of gay rights imply that the homosexual impulse is so strong in so many people that only constant vigilance embodied in laws, taboos, and prohibitions will serve as a floodgate to stem the homosexual tides that threaten to drown the human race!

A second flaw in the argument of many who oppose any protection for gay and lesbian persons is the unproven assumption that homosexual behavior is harmful or destructive to individuals or society and that homosexuality will increase if we protect homosexual persons and/or condone homosexual behavior. Contrary to popular belief, no society or culture, including Greece, Rome, Sodom and Gommorah, has ever collapsed because of homosexual behavior. Societies and cultures react differently to the phenomenon of homosexuality. At certain periods in both Greece and Rome, high culture flourished alongside a certain tolerance of, and openness to, rather carefully circumscribed expressions of homosexuality. No society has ever held homosexuality to be an ideal. Sodom and Gommorah were destroyed for gross injustices toward the poor, for inhospitality, and perhaps, for gang rape, a reprehensible crime whether homosexual or heterosexual (Bailey, 1975).

There is no proof that those societies which tolerate certain forms of homosexuality evidence a higher percentage of gay and lesbian persons. Likewise those countries that exhibit particularly hostile and punitive attitudes towards homosexuality show no decrease in the percentage of homosexually oriented individuals. In cities and states where protective legislation for gay and lesbian citizens has been enacted, there has been no increase in the homosexual population.

It might be proven, however, that those geographic areas which respect the rights of homosexual citizens would be a natural draw for lesbian and gay people because their lives could be much easier in such a climate. But the fear often voiced in small towns across the country is similar. "If we pass this gay rights bill our town will become a gay mecca." While gay and lesbian people might move to San Francisco, Washington, D.C., or even New York in significant numbers for educational and career reasons, it is doubtful that civil rights legislation in Eugene, Oregon; Norristown, Pennsylvania; or Maywood, New Jersey, would precipitate a major influx of homosexual people to those places! What such legislation will do is to make life for gay and lesbian people already living in certain locales more secure and more pleasant.

With the advent of the HIV-AIDS crisis, the argument against gay rights legislation, that homosexual activity causes demonstrable damage both to society and to individuals, has received apparent confirmation for some people. Apart from confusing protection for orientation with protection for sexual behavior, the simple response is twofold: First of all, globally at least, HIV-AIDS is a numerically heterosexual disease. Secondly, it is a virus that causes AIDS, not sexual behavior. Society has never outlawed heterosexual intercourse because of sexually transmitted diseases. Society has, however, taken both medical and legal steps to curtail and eliminate such diseases. In the same way, society can and should take steps to control and eliminate HIV-AIDS, but not by disenfranchising ten percent of the population of their sexuality.

Such steps should not include policies and procedures that threaten the privacy and basic human rights of individuals. Indiscriminate mandatory testing, imposed quarantine, denial of insurance coverage or benefits, and public listing or disclosure of people with HIV-AIDS are invasions of the basic right to privacy. However, there is a serious personal and communal responsibility for everyone to alter their sexual practices not only for their own personal interests, but also as part of an effort to prevent the increase of HIV-AIDS.

Employment

In proposing legislation in the area of employment, there are some issues that need to be specifically addressed. Protection in employment generally implies legislation that makes it illegal either to fire someone solely on the grounds of a homosexual orientation or to refuse to hire an individual for the same reason. Most of the discrimination that gay and lesbian people face in this area has to do with being fired rather than being hired. Few job applications today inquire specifically about an applicant's sexual orientation. Some military and government agencies, however, do scrutinize this area of an applicant's life more than others in the interviewing process, although the practice is being challenged legally.

What most gay and lesbian people fear is possible dismissal from a position simply for being discovered. Even in those cities and towns that have enacted anti-discrimination ordinances or in those firms that have incorporated similar clauses in their policies, lesbian and gay people often find themselves in a Catch-22 situation. If such an individual wishes to fight to retain a job, then he or she eventually has to initiate a formal complaint or undertake a hearing or a court trial. In either case, there is little chance of preserving one's anonymity. For the person who does not want his or her homosexuality a matter of public record, such protection is not very comforting.

Military personnel officers Lieutenant Leonard Matlovitch and Ensign Vernon Berg and school teacher Joseph Acanfora are individuals who felt it more important to fight for principle than to protect their anonymity. The fundamental insight underlying job protection is that a homosexual orientation is never sufficient reason for depriving a person of his or her ordinary rights to employment, advancement, and equal benefits. Orientation, whether homosexual or heterosexual, is a personal and private matter and, ordinarily, has no effect on a person's job performance unless an individual chooses to make it an issue.

But what of homosexual behavior? External behavior that is not a matter of public record should not, of itself, be the basis for discriminating against employees. Even if an employer learns about the private sexual behavior of an employee, that information ought not to be used against the employee unless it can be proved that the behavior in question seriously affects the ability of the person to fulfill the duties associated with his or her position.

It is often objected that it should not be illegal to fire gay or lesbian persons because of the danger of blackmail, for example, in some sensitive government intelligence-related positions. Yet the only reason at present that supports blackmail is the fact that society judges homosexuality so negatively. If, in fact, homosexuality were regarded by society as a variant of human sexuality for at least ten percent of the population, then the very grounds for any blackmail opportunity would be eliminated. No one would have to fear being known as a homosexual person if there were no stigma or opprobrium attached to this sexual identity; there would be no possibility for blackmail attempts or threats. In fact, gay and lesbian individuals who are already out of the closet claim that the grounds for blackmail, i.e., making a fact public, have been eliminated.

Gay and Lesbian Teachers

One of the most sensitive and emotional topics about gay rights and job protection involves gay and lesbian school teachers and child care workers. The concern about teachers is less a fear about child molestation or even seduction because current statistics show that the large majority of such cases involve heterosexual offenders. An equally valid concern, however, is the question of healthy lesbian or gay role models for young students.

At the bottom of this question, however, is the unspoken fear that the sexual orientation of the teacher might have some effect on the sexual orientation of the student. If the sexuality of the adult did influence the sexual orientation of the child, then how does one account for the ten percent of the children who, having been exposed all their lives to heterosexual role models from parents, teachers, clergy, and others, nevertheless developed as homosexual individuals?

While healthy role models for impressionable young people are of crucial importance to parents and educators, there is an additional need for healthy role models for those students who are developing with homosexual orientations. Although gay and lesbian students will always comprise the minority in the educational and social settings of our society, their needs and problems are no less worthy of our serious personal concern and institutional resources.

Civil rights protection for jobs such as teaching does not mean that society might not have to dismiss some gay or lesbian employees because of inappropriate or unprofessional behavior. But if this is the case, then the problem is one of a serious disturbance of the public order (of the workplace, for example) and not simply one of homosexual orientation. The restrictions placed upon homosexual teachers, in fairness, ought to be the same as those placed on heterosexual teachers. Without legal protection of their orientation, gay and lesbian teachers live in constant fear of discovery and subsequent dismissal. No matter how talented or how dedicated to their profession, their careers can end in disaster simply for acknowledging honestly their human sexual identity. Teachers, students, and the entire educational system would be much better off if mature and responsible lesbian and gay teachers could be relieved of this unnecessary burden.

The psychologist Carl Jung theorized that homosexual people

are drawn, almost instinctively, to those professions that require a special capacity for nurturing, healing, and growth of others. Jung (1959) observed that they are often "endowed with a wealth of religious feelings, which help to bring the _ecclesia spiritualis_ into reality" (vol. 9, part 1, p. 86). Among the professions where there is an unusually high percentage of lesbian women and gay men are nursing, the clergy, and teaching. No one will deny that the teaching profession has historically embraced large numbers of gay and lesbian people and many will admit that among the most creative teachers in their own lives have been homosexually oriented ones. These are living proof of the ability of gay and lesbian teachers and others in similar positions to exercise their professional responsibilities in a manner that justifies legal protection against arbitrary dismissal.

With the recent spate of child sexual abuse coming to light in this country, there is a need to separate an adult and mature homosexual orientation from the psychological disturbance called pedophilia, which manifests itself both in heterosexual and homosexual child abuse. Employers for child care institutions have a right and responsibility to inquire into the backgrounds of potential employees to determine if there is any history of pedophilia. They have the right to dismiss employees who evidence such behavior and to investigate reasonably founded suspicions or charges. But in all these cases, it must be remembered, the issue is pedophilia, not homosexuality.

Adoption and Child Custody

Two other issues require additional comment because they raise concerns from people opposed to gay rights. These are the issues of custody rights, foster care, and adoption by gay and lesbian individuals or same-sex couples. There are no legal precedents established in either of these issues. Individual jurisdictions, states, and agencies render decisions and make policies based on a variety of circumstances including prevailing community mores and the political makeup of the geographical area in which the decisions are being made.

Individuals and groups working for legal reform in these areas assert that the simple fact of being gay or lesbian is not, in and of itself, sufficient reason for denying foster care, adoption, or custody rights.

Battles have been waged, especially by lesbian mothers, across the nation to protect their right to retain and raise children after legal separation or divorce. Gay fathers also seek court orders to keep their children, claiming, at times, that they are more competent to raise the children than the biological mother.

The question that is asked in all of these cases is what effect will the homosexual orientation of the parent, foster-parent, or adoptive-parent have on the sexuality of the child. The younger the child is, the more concern that is expressed. There is no proof that the sexual orientation of the parent affects that of the child. A related question raised by some judges has to do with the moral tone or moral climate of the home in which one of the parents is lesbian or gay. For example, if there is a strong belief that the homosexual lifestyle is "immoral," then the judgment will generally go against the lesbian or gay person who is automatically not considered as a fit parent. This is usually true when there are two homosexual individuals present in the home, but also even in the case of a single gay or lesbian person who applies for foster care, adoption, or child custody.

There are no simple answers to any of these complex questions. What gay and lesbian advocates suggest is that the law should not automatically decide these cases simply on the basis of the sexual orientation of the parent. A same-sex, responsible, and stable male couple would make a much better environment, for example, for raising a child than would a home with an alcoholic, abusive mother. Two lesbian women raising children from a previous marriage is a much healthier social situation than awarding custody of children to a biological father who is a drug or gambling addict.

The age, maturity, and wishes of the child need to be considered seriously in making such a judgment. While some children might be able to cope with the situation of living in a home with one or two lesbian or gay parents, the same situation might cause great stress for others. Even those who thrive in such situations also need help in coping with misunderstanding, ridicule, and even rejection by classmates, friends, and peers.

While the ideal home environment for sexual and social maturing has traditionally been the presence of a heterosexual male and female, the instances of heterosexual family breakdown, child abuse, incest, and other serious problems make us less able to judge negatively the parenting skills of lesbian and gay individuals.

The real needs for the healthy growth of children are nonpossessive love, responsible affection, religious values, and caring discipline. The ability to embody these qualities does not depend on one's sexual orientation. Given the number of unwanted children and the proven ability of many homosexual people to provide good environments, society cannot afford to be blinded by unfounded biases and unproven assumptions about the "dangers" of placing adopted and foster-care children with lesbian and gay individuals and couples.

Conclusion

The struggle for gay rights will continue and expand in the coming years. This chapter has not touched on many other civil rights for which some gay and lesbian people are working. All of them are both emotional and controversial. Should same-sex couples be afforded the same rights as heterosexuals to civil and religious marriage ceremonies? Should individuals be entitled to palimony or something comparable to the support that people receive following a divorce? Should homosexuality be taught in the schools simply as an alternative lifestyle? Should students have gay clubs in school as African American and Hispanic students have ethnic clubs and be allowed to take a same-sex partner to the senior prom? Should gay and lesbian employees have a legal right to exactly the same work benefits, such as health and insurance coverage, for their spouses as married heterosexual partners already enjoy? Positive responses to these questions require a much different definition of both marriage and family than society has been willing to make. Legal protection for jobs and housing for lesbian and gay people might be among the least controversial or threatening topics for many people to consider and even support. Other issues of procreation through modern technology like artificial insemination, test tube babies, third-party semen donors, and surrogate motherhood all raise serious ethical and legal questions about personal dignity, the nature of human sexuality, and the rights and limitations of human reproduction.

The outcome of the movement for gay and lesbian rights is unpredictable. Like any social movement it will experience times of victory and acceptance and times of social rejection and defeat, sometimes simultaneously. The political, religious, and social climate all interact with the gay and lesbian liberation movement both to modify it and, in turn, to be modified by it. It is doubtful that the gains won thus far will be lost or that the social tolerance for homosexuality will drastically change. Legal equality will not necessarily bring about personal or social acceptance. But at the very least, legal equality will prevent individuals and groups from acting out their irrational fears against gay and lesbian people by firing them from jobs, refusing them accommodations, or denying them the opportunity to become foster parents or adoptive parents.

Society need not fear homosexuality. It is neither a threat to the family nor an attack on marital values. But society has much to fear from bigotry, ignorance, and hostility as responses to a form of human sexual identity that is different from the majority. If we have learned our lesson from the experiences of generations past who fled to our country for religious and other freedoms, we will hesitate to deny or restrict the responsible sexual freedom of a minority of those who live among us and who deserve our respect and friendship.

–2–

Debunking the Myths

Along with the cries of liberation from women, African Americans, Chicanos, Native Americans, and other oppressed groups come public declarations of independence from America's lesbian and gay communities. The significant departure from the bondage of oppression can be traced back to the 1969 Stonewall Rebellion, which was described in the previous chapter. The violent resistance of the Stonewall was much more than the spontaneous outburst of a small group of angry people tired of being treated as third-class citizens. The action symbolized more universal feeling slowly, but steadily, growing in America's gay and lesbian community, no longer content in being forced to lead a dual life of straight by day and gay by night.

The leaders of America's newest vocal minority, conservatively estimated at more than 22 million people, were chanting "Two, four, six, eight; gay is just as good as straight." No longer must lesbian and gay people feel they should hide in the closet, the leaders said. In a 1971 *New York Times Magazine* article, Merle Miller told what it was like to be a homosexual. A Los Angeles student, just out of his closet, commented, "Now that everyone knows, I really feel at ease with myself for the first time in my life" (Young, 1971).

Coming out is bound to have a profound impact on a lesbian or gay person's life. Lesbian and gay people should not have to live with the fear of discovery that may result in rejection by friends or the threat of job loss. Society's attitudes are slowly changing. To change social attitudes radically is a common goal of the gay and lesbian organizations, which have been mushrooming steadily since 1950. The number of these organizations soared dramatically in the late 1960s and early 1970s. Today there are independent gay and lesbian groups on most of the nation's leading university campuses, including many Catholic institutions, such as Georgetown University, the Catholic University of America, and the University of Notre Dame. A major thrust of these groups is attitudinal change; but attitudes can change only when people accept exposure to new ideas, accurate facts, and a willingness to investigate all sides of a question. Education, as a conveyor of truth, plays a significant role in reshaping people's attitudes. Education about homosexuality must replace stereotypes with the truth, myths with the realities. What are the myths that hamper and limit lesbian and gay persons?

A common and long held myth in American society says that gay men are effeminate, limp-wristed individuals. A revealing episode of the once popular television show "All in the Family" showed Archie Bunker meeting a noticeably effeminate friend of his son-in-law. Seeking more "masculine" companionship, Archie visits the local tavern and complains of this "queer" to a decidedly masculine-looking, regular patron, a former football player. After patiently listening to Archie's tale, the man reveals that he himself is gay. Archie's stunned and incredulous look mirrors the surprise of most of the American public when they come to realize that gay men are not necessarily effeminate.

The Institute for Sex Research at Indiana University estimated that only 15% of gay males are easily recognizable, and only five per cent of lesbian women are identifiable as "butch" or masculine in appearance (Jones, 1966). The gay doctor in the British film "Sunday, Bloody Sunday" and the divorced man and his lover in the television production "That Certain Summer," were certainly not the lisping, mincing brand of gay male that American society has grown accustomed to expect. There are, undoubtedly, effeminate gay men and masculine-type lesbian women, but these constitute only a small minority of the gay and lesbian population. These individuals, as well as transvestites, are most likely to come into public view, and consequently play a large part in forming public opinion about lesbian and gay people. Dr. Evelyn Hooker, an eminent psychologist who chaired the Task Force on Homosexuality for the National Institute of Mental Health, concluded that there is no essential relation between effeminacy of body build, manner, or speech, and homosexuality.

Psychiatry was long considered the traditional archenemy of lesbian and gay people until the early 1970s. Most psychiatrists viewed homosexuality as a neurotic disorder. But many psychiatrists began to doubt the validity of this assumption. Hoffman (1969) conducted a non-clinical study and found that there were a significant number of gay people who, by reasonable clinical criteria, could not be considered mentally ill. Pomeroy (1969), a prominent New York psychologist and staff member of the Institute for

Sex Research for 20 years, wrote, "If my concept of homosexuality were developed from my practice, I would probably concur in thinking of it as an illness. I have seen no homosexual man or woman in that practice who was not troubled, emotionally upset, or neurotic. On the other hand, if my concept of marriage in the U.S. were based on my practice, I would have to conclude that marriages are fraught with strife and conflict, and that heterosexuality is an illness. In my 20 years of research in the field of sex, I have seen many homosexuals who were happy, who were practicing and conscientious members of their community, and who were stable, productive, warm, relaxed, and efficient. Except for the fact that they were homosexual, they could be considered normal by any definition" (p. 13).

To resist the pressures of a society in which traditionally a lesbian or gay person was branded a sinner by religion, judged a criminal by law, and diagnosed as sick by the medical profession, she or he had to be a very strong personality indeed. A heterosexual person of average stamina might very well collapse emotionally in the face of such hostilities. Rather than point to lesbian or gay individuals who are psychologically maladjusted as confirmation that homosexuality is a disease, we should marvel that so many gay and lesbian people are psychologically sound.

In a classic study, Hooker (1957) found 30 gay men who, she felt, were reasonably well-adjusted and were not in treatment, and 30 heterosexual men who were matched for age, education, and I.Q. She gave all 60 males a battery of psychological tests, including the Rorschach and the Thematic Apperception Test. She submitted the results for analysis to three of her colleagues who did not know which of the tests had been given to the gay men and which to the heterosexual men. The clinicians who interpreted the results were unable to distinguish any significant difference between the two groups tested. The general conclusion was that there is no inherent connection between homosexual orientation and clinical symptoms of mental illness.

Thompson, McCandless, and Strickland (1971) conducted a study of personal adjustment with groups of white, well-educated gay men and lesbian women. They were matched for age, sex, and education with heterosexual controls. The results indicated that the lesbian and gay group did not differ in any way from heterosexuals in defensiveness, personal adjustment, self-confidence, or self-evaluation. Similar results were reported by Chang and Block (1960).

All of this research, plus much more lobbying from the lesbian and gay movement, induced the board of trustees of the American Psychiatric Association [APA] in December 1973 to declassify homosexuality as a mental illness. Because of some strong opposition to this move, the issue was placed in referendum in the spring of 1974. The majority of the voting members of the APA concurred with the board's decision. In 1974, the American Psychological Association took a similar stand of treating homosexuality as an alternative lifestyle, as did the National Association of Social Workers. In the 1990s most workers in the helping professions no longer consider homosexuality a deviancy, but rather view it as a variant form of sexual expression.

Another myth, quite widespread on a popular level, says that a homosexual orientation is caused by a confluence of factors in the parent-child relationship, which are manifested in a domineering or overprotective mother and a weak or absent father. This is the classic psychoanalytic explanation of the origins of homosexuality. It is no longer held by a majority of experts in the field of sexual identity because many heterosexual persons have the same family constellation.

A recent study, which received wide media coverage, suggests that sexual orientation among gay men may be related to the size of one section of the hypothalamus in the brain (LeVay, 1991). If confirmed, the results would show that a homosexual orientation is biologically based and not the result of upbringing. Although such a finding would corroborate what many lesbian and gay persons have said about their orientation, many of them expressed caution and even skepticism about the San Diego study, which contains serious methodological questions. For example, all of the 19 homosexual men in the study died of AIDS. It is possible that the difference in brain structure of these men is related to the disease rather than to sexual orientation. Furthermore, the 16 subjects to which the homosexual brain structure was compared were *presumed* to be heterosexual. It is possible that some of them were bisexual or homosexual. LeVay acknowledges that the existence of "exceptions" in his sample "hints at the possibility that sexual orientation, although an important variable, may not be the sole determinant" (p. 1036). There is need for further biologically based studies with larger sample sizes and more controlled research designs.

For almost a century researchers have tried to solve the mystery of the origins of a homosexual orientation. We know that there is no different chromosomal structure between lesbian or gay individuals and heterosexual persons, as some had once surmised (Pare, 1956). Other studies testing biologically based theories, such as those involving hormonal levels, have been conducted with such small sample sizes that they have proved inconclusive. Even if a correlation is found between levels of hormone and sexual orientation, we still will not have established a causal relationship. Do varied levels of hormones produce different sexual orientations or do different sexual orientations result in different levels of hormones? Perhaps there is a third or even fourth factor indirectly influencing the development of both.

Other theories claim that environment is responsible for a

homosexual orientation. One way of testing an environmental theory involves longitudinal studies of monozygotic or identical twins. Since identical twins are the product of the same zygote or the same hereditary make-up, any differences in adult twins are due to environmental factors. The results of studies involving identical twins reared apart have varied. Kallmann (1952a, 1952b) found that the sexual orientation of 40 pairs of monozygotic twins were similar, even when reared apart. Klintworth (1962) and others, however, found cases of identical twins, one of whom is homosexual and the other heterosexual.

After decades of research into the causes of homosexuality, we are still left with a big question mark. A current theory being explored by the Kinsey Institute for Sex Research in Indiana can be summarized as follows: There is no single explanation for the development of any sexual orientation. Each person's orientation is influenced by a host of environmental and biological factors. The orientation of those persons at the extremes of the Kinsey sexual orientation rating scale, i.e., an exclusive or strongly predominant homosexual or heterosexual orientation (Kinsey categories 0, 1, 5, and 6), is probably more influenced by biological factors than by environmental ones. For those persons who are strictly bisexual or whose orientation borders on bisexuality (Kinsey categories 2, 3, and 4), environmental factors most likely play a more significant role than biological ones in sexual orientation development. This theory is an attempt to understand the origins of a heterosexual as well as a homosexual orientation. The important issue may not be *why* we develop sexually as we do but that we develop as whole and healthy sexual persons with a proper appreciation and respect for our sexual natures and the sexuality of others.

There are many other myths about homosexuality that need to be eradicated by sound education. The American public all too frequently views gay men as pedophiles, those who are sexually involved with youths under the age of 18. Each year, a small number of homosexual males, less than one percent of the total gay population, are arrested for seducing male youths. Each year, an even greater number of heterosexual males are arrested for seducing young girls. Yet the public does not conclude that heterosexuality is a perversion, but rightly concludes that some heterosexuals suffer from this maladjustment. Most lesbian and gay people hold values similar to their heterosexual counterparts regarding child molestation. The only logical conclusion can be that *some* homosexual people are also pedophiles.

The Institute for Sex Research published a massive volume on sex offenders, which showed that those who were arrested for sexual offenses with boys under 16 were generally bisexual (Gebhard, Gagnon, Pomeroy and Christensen, 1965). Such men were preoccupied with satisfying sexual urges with the young, regardless of their gender. Particularly in the last decade, there has been an increasing interest in child sexual abuse for the purpose of exploring its nature, causes, extent, legal aspects, and ultimately, some treatment programs for the victims and perpetrators. Some of us may be surprised to learn that approximately 90% of child sexual abusers are male. How many of us realize that the typical perpetrator of sexual attacks is a young, middle class, well-educated, white, heterosexual male? He usually has a good-paying job, eventually marries and gains the trust of a female minor whom he victimizes (Rossetti, 1990). As more and more evidence is documented, the erroneous belief that confuses child molestation with homosexuality is more obviously exposed.

Another myth claims that all lesbian and gay people are promiscuous. It is probably fair to assert that many gay males in the visible gay subculture are promiscuous. In present-day American culture, heterosexual relationships are undergoing deep stress regarding permanence. However, we do not thereby conclude that heterosexuality is undesirable. Similarly, we should not make any sweeping judgments about homosexuality or all lesbian and gay people because of some promiscuity in the gay subculture.

People, of whatever sexual orientation, are experiencing difficulty in maintaining their love relationships. The lesbian or gay person, unlike his or her heterosexual counterpart, lacks most of the social and cultural factors that tend to provide a supportive atmosphere for a stable relationship. A gay executive, for example, cannot bring his lover to a formal company dinner dance at the local country club, nor can a lesbian professor invite her lover to the university's Christmas party. Heterosexual marriages are sanctioned by churches, and even rewarded by the state. A same-sex couple receives no tax benefits or reduced family rates for excursions and sundry entertainment. The strong social components that reinforce heterosexual marriages are simply not available to the same-sex couple. Despite the great social pressures they must endure, many lesbian and gay people have been able to maintain a stable, permanent relationship for many years.

For a lesbian or gay person, housing and job discrimination is not infrequent. Many social and church facilities are barred from their use because "respectable" people do not desire to associate with them. Such reactions are reminiscent of the white, middle-class citizen who passionately denied feelings of prejudice while keeping African Americans far removed from his or her neighborhood and church.

Many "broad-minded" heterosexuals complain, "I don't mind fags as long as they keep quiet about it. They don't have to tell anyone." Jack Baker, a 29-year-old law student and president of the graduate student body at the University of Minnesota in 1970, caused a stir by applying for a marriage licence in the seventies. Learning of Baker's homosexuality, his brother rejected him and said Baker was no longer welcome in his house. Still, Baker claimed, "All this hypocrisy and double life is a lot of nonsense and there just comes a time when you've had enough of it" (Tobin and Wicker, 1972, p. 140).

The criminal status of homosexuality in most states of the U.S. and throughout the world likewise does not foster stable same-sex relationships. Laws used to persecute lesbian and gay persons can be traced back to the fourth century when Christianity became the dominant religion of the Roman Empire. By 1991, most major Western countries had discarded archaic laws prohibiting same-sex acts between consenting adults, excepting half the states in the U.S. Although most existing laws prohibiting anal and oral intercourse apply equally to opposite-sex and same-sex couples, the laws have been enforced almost exclusively against gay men. In 9 states, these laws apply only to homosexual persons. Legal reform in this area is a major goal of gay and lesbian organizations. The major policy reason for abolishing existing laws against same-sex behavior is simply that private acts between consenting adults are matters of private morality and are not properly the concern of the state. The movement to rescind these state sodomy statutes suffered a major setback in June 1986 when the Supreme Court upheld the right of the State of Georgia to make same-sex acts a criminal offense. However, in 1990, retired Supreme Court Justice Lewis Powell, the swing vote in the decision, publicly stated, "I think I probably made a mistake in that one" (Marcus, 1990, p. A3).

Not all societies view homosexuality as a taboo. A study of 193 world cultures reported by Hock and Zubin (1949) showed that male homosexuality was accepted by 28% of the cultures and rejected by 14%, while 58% showed partial acceptance or equivocation. Pomeroy (1969) reported that 53% of 225 American Indian cultures accepted male homosexuality, while only 24% of the cultures rejected it. Although the cowboys of the Wild West in the nineteenth century scorned effeminate men, they apparently widely practiced same-sex behavior. Pomeroy contends that overt homosexuality was probably more common among this group than among any other group of males in the U.S.

Still, twentieth-century American society is less than tolerant of homosexuality. An anthropologist recounts, "Among the generality of Americans, homosexuality is regarded not with distaste, disgust, or abhorrence, but with panic; it is seen as an immediate and personal threat...The lives of most American men are bounded, and their interests drastically curtailed, by this constant necessity to prove to their fellows, and to themselves, that they are not...homosexuals. It is difficult to exaggerate the prevalence of this unconscious fear" (Gorer, 1964, pp. 128-129).

After years of research in the field of sex, the biologist and sexual researcher Alfred Kinsey concluded that human beings cannot be classified simply as heterosexual or homosexual. Kinsey devised a seven-point scale ranging from "exclusively homosexual" to "exclusively heterosexual." An individual may be located at different points on the scale at different periods of his or her life. Kinsey (1948) explained that human beings "do not represent two discrete populations, heterosexual and homosexual. The world is not to be divided into sheep and goats....It is a fundamental of taxonomy that nature rarely deals with discrete categories. Only the human mind invents categories and tries to force facts into separate pigeonholes. The living world is a continuum in each and every one of its aspects. The sooner we learn of this concerning human sexual behavior, the sooner we shall reach a sound understanding of the realities of sex" (p. 639).

Education must replace homosexual myths with homosexual realities. Most lesbian and gay people do not fit the stereotyped images. Very few gay persons are child-molesters. Not all lesbian or gay individuals are promiscuous. A lesbian or gay person is more similar to a heterosexual of common educational and socioeconomic background than to another lesbian or gay person of different educational and socioeconomic background. The only thing all lesbian and gay people have in common is their sexual, erotic orientation.

Attitudinal change can occur only through exposure, contact, education, and confrontation with the lived truth. Barbara Gittings (1969), a lesbian spokesperson prominent in the early years of the movement, observed very aptly, "The only way to break down misunderstanding and prejudice is by meeting and working with and learning to understand people" (p. 151). But then, most people probably have met and worked with lesbian and gay people without even realizing it.

–3–

What Is Natural?

Since 1971 I have worked in church ministry for lesbian and gay Catholics. Much of the time has been devoted to providing educational opportunities for heterosexual people to discuss the sensitive topic of homosexuality in a calm, reasoned, and impassioned way. When I have met resistance from well-meaning heterosexual people to accepting lesbian and gay individuals as persons, the bottom line has usually been, "But homosexuality is just unnatural." I try to pursue the conversation logically by asking them to explain their statement and to define, as best they can, what they mean by the words "unnatural" and "natural."

Over the years, their explanations and definitions have varied. I am convinced that people have unconsciously absorbed from the dominant culture a deep-seated feeling of antipathy toward homosexuality for which they have tried, usually unsuccessfully, to provide a semblance of intelligent argument. For a good part of my adult life, I also unquestioningly assumed that homosexuality was unnatural. But from meeting thousands of lesbian and gay people over the years, from reading reliable research in the field, and from reflecting on what it means to be natural, I am now convinced that homosexual and bisexual feelings and behaviors are just as natural as heterosexual ones.

In this chapter, I shall present some of the reasons or arguments I have heard on both sides of the question. I shall examine what it means to be "natural" and, in doing so, shall draw upon historical, anthropological, psychological, and biological evidence. That the main stumbling block to my argument comes from theological and philosophical discourse demonstrates to me that these disciplines either have failed to keep abreast of scientific developments or have willfully ignored current findings in order to legitimize a preconceived notion of divine intent for the human order. How can I say that bisexual and homosexual feelings are as natural as heterosexual ones? What does it mean to be "natural"? Let me consider the definition of the word from various disciplines.

History

Goethe once wrote that homosexuality can be considered natural because it is as old as the human race itself. Some people, such as Goethe, would say that something is natural if it has existed and continues to exist over time and place. This is a definition of "natural" that I have heard among a number of professors in academic circles. History and anthropology give us some information to make a judgment about homosexuality vis-a-vis this definition.

History would certainly affirm Goethe's belief. It is fairly well-known that particular societies at different historical times socially approved of homosexual and bisexual liaisons. Between the eighth and second centuries before the Christian era, Greek art and literature assumed that virtually everyone responded at different times both to homosexual and to heterosexual stimuli. Such an attitude was implicit in the philosophical and nonphilosophical writings of the day. In Plato's *Symposium*, the guests at a dinner party take turns delivering speeches in praise of Eros, the god of love. Most of the examples used by the speakers are homosexual. In expounding his own view of eros in the work, Plato describes a beautiful male responding to the beauty of another male, and not to a female, as the starting point of his philosophical understanding of ideal beauty. Probably because homosexual relations were so commonly accepted, Plutarch, another Greek writer, in his *Dialogue on Love*, had to argue passionately in defense of the naturalness of heterosexual love.

Rowse (1977) has documented numerous cases of homosexual people throughout history. Let us consider only a few of these. The famous twelfth-century English king, Richard the Lionhearted, seems to have been bisexual, though obviously preferring the company of his male minstrel. The coronation festivities of the fourteenth-century English king, Edward II, were almost halted by Edward's conspicuous attention for Piers Gaveston, his constant male companion whom, historians say, "he adored." When powerful barons murdered his beloved Gaveston, the king could only take the body, grieve intensely, and pray for his loved one's soul. From his passionate love letters to a fellow monk and from his close male attachments, historians believe that the medieval scholar Erasmus was also homosexually oriented.

The Renaissance genius Leonardo da Vinci wrote that heterosexual intercourse was "so ugly that, if it were not for the beauty of faces and the liberation of the spirit, the species would lose its humanity," i.e., the human race would cease to propagate

(Rowse, 1977, p. 13). At age 24, the reserved and aristocratic da Vinci was accused of having sex with a 17-year-old male and imprisoned for two months. More withdrawn and mysterious than ever after his release, da Vinci engaged a handsome, irresistible youth as an apprentice and taught him to paint. Although the young man stole from his master as well as from his master's clients, da Vinci overlooked his faults because of his strong attachment to the youth. The man eventually left da Vinci but the master painter was to find happiness in the devotion of another man who remained faithful to him until da Vinci's death.

Although he was da Vinci's contemporary, Michelangelo di Lodovico Buonarroti could not have been more unlike da Vinci in temperament and personality. While Leonardo was calm, courteous, and an introvert, Michelangelo was abrupt, aggressive, impatient; the two men disliked each other. Unmarried like da Vinci, Michelangelo often celebrated the male nude body in his sculptures, paintings, and drawings. His preference for males was well known during his lifetime although there is no documentation concerning his sexual practice. After his death his love poems to Cavalieri, who became the passion of his life, were altered so that they appeared to be addressed to a woman.

Although a host of eminent historical figures were homosexual, most of those known to us are male because most of our religious, literary, and political information has been written by men about men and for other men to read. Only in more modern times have women produced historical records of themselves. Despite this significant handicap, historical data do indicate that lesbian women have existed, though certainly more hidden, throughout the ages.

Harris (1978) points out that there is a "lesbian silence" (p. 257) of approximately twenty-four centuries from the time of Sappho (about 613 B.C.E.) to the end of the nineteenth century. Patriarchal society inhibited any literary expression of lesbianism. Before there can be literature from any group, there must first be a cultural identity or a set of common characteristics that bonds the group members together.

The word "lesbian" derives from the ancient Greek poet Sappho who lived on the island of Lesbos with her community of female admirers. During her lifetime, Sappho's poetry was renowned throughout the Greek world. In her honor, statues were erected and coins were minted. Even a century after her ceremonious burial, Socrates and Plato publicly praised her. But several centuries later, the social independence of women was being curtailed. Sappho began to be portrayed as a prostitute, which she never was. Eventually, Sappho was ridiculed and censured. With the influence of the Christian state, Sappho's poems were publicly burned in the fourth century and again in the eleventh century (Klaich, 1974).

The end of the lesbian silence is owed to the outspoken Natalie Clifford Barney and Renée Vivien, who lived at the end of the nineteenth century in France. Their conviction that lesbianism is a valid, even superior, lifestyle for women was accepted only in the small circle of society in which they lived. It would not find social acceptance until the 1960s. Renée Vivien would have produced more novels had she not died at the young age of thirty-two of self-imposed starvation. Her friend and lover, Natalie Barney, is remembered more for her extraordinary person than for her memoirs, fictional prose, and poetry. Barney rejected sex roles, monogamy, possessiveness, jealousy, and everything she thought of as bourgeois morality.

In the twentieth century, the only literature of lesbian women to become mainstream are the works of Radcliffe Hall, Djuna Barnes, and Gertrude Stein. Harris (1978) attributes the popularity of the first two authors not only to their genius but also to their stance against male supremacy, their request for tolerance of lesbianism, their belief in God, and, in the case of Barnes, the patronage of T. S. Eliot. Stein, while she would not name herself a lesbian, has been acclaimed by the feminist community for her female-centered work. In film, art, and prose, the lesbian and gay community has celebrated the thirty-nine years of devotion of Alice B. Toklas to Gertrude Stein.

Other lesbian writers of fiction and poetry include Jane Rule, May Sarton, Vita Sackville-West, and Rita Mae Brown. Recent books are beginning to describe the lesbian lifestyles of Rosa Bonheur, Willa Cather, Amy Lowell, Emily Dickinson, and others (Richards, 1990). Some lesbian women, such as George Sand, assumed male pseudonyms in their careers. Others, such as Georgia O'Keeffe, very comfortably lived a bisexual lifestyle in the circles in which they traveled (Eisler, 1991). In the early 1970s, four women singers and actresses declared they were bisexual: Joan Baez, Janis Joplin, Lily Tomlin, and Maria Schneider. Biographers and historians are slowly uncovering evidence to suggest or confirm the lesbian preferences of women formerly assumed to be exclusively heterosexual.

Anthropology

Lesbian and gay individuals have existed at all times throughout history. They have also existed in almost all cultures that anthropologists have studied. In those cultures where homosexuality has not been observed, anthropologists point out that language and communication problems may have obscured evidence of them. Moreover, those societies in which no same-sex behavior is evident are very sparsely populated ones, such as the Alorese in the mountains of Timor. We would expect that in such close knit groupings it would be difficult for individuals to engage in relationships disapproved of by the group.

Homosexual practices were condoned and even encouraged

among the ancient Greeks and Romans. The ancient Celts, Scandinavians, Egyptians, Etruscans, Cretans, Carthagenians, and Sumerians accepted same-sex behavior. The greatest approval of homosexuality in ancient times came from the lands surrounding the Tigris-Euphrates and the Nile River and the Mediterranean Sea. With the exception of the Hebrews and perhaps the Assyrians, the ancient cultures of the Mediterranean implicitly sanctioned the same-sex instincts of their people.

In the past, the Far East also tolerated homosexuality and bisexuality. From ancient to modern times, same-sex behavior has been acceptable in China and Japan. In China, where male brothels were common, boys were trained for prostitution by their parents. In Japan during the feudal period, male homosexual love was considered more "manly" than heterosexual love. Male geishas in teahouses were prevalent until the middle of the nineteenth century and still existed until they were suppressed at the end of World War II by the American occupation forces. Today lesbian and gay people in both Japan and China remain more hidden (Churchill, 1967).

In some cultures homosexuality is identified with sex-role stereotyping. Among the Koniag of Alaska, the Largo of East Africa, the Tanala of Madagascar, and the Chukchee of Siberia, some males are raised from early childhood to perform female tasks and to dress as females. Known as the "berdache," such a male often becomes the "wife" of an important man in the community and lives with him, but the berdache may have heterosexual affairs with a mistress and father children. The berdache often enjoys a considerable amount of social prestige and assumes a position of power in the community. He usually becomes a shaman, a kind of priest, medicine man, or religious figure, who is believed to possess supernatural powers that may be transmitted by sexual relations.

An example of socially expected and approved bisexuality involving a large segment of the male population is found among the Siwans of Africa. Both married and unmarried men are expected to have bisexual affairs and those males who do not engage in same-sex behavior are considered odd. In a number of cultures, such as the Keraki of New Guinea and the Kiwai, homosexual behavior is sanctioned as part of male puberty rites. In a detailed study of cultural data from 76 societies, 64% of the cultures surveyed approved of some form of homosexual behavior and considered it normal and socially acceptable for at least some members of the community (Ford & Beach, 1951).

So it seems to be clear from historical and anthropological data that homosexuality is natural if "natural" is defined to be existence over time and place. But there are other ways to consider the meaning of this word.

Psychology

A second definition of the word "natural" is psychologically based. From a psychological perspective, an action is considered natural if it originates from an instinct, impulse, or drive. An involuntary want or need coming from within an organism is natural to that organism. If such an instinctive urge is not impeded, an individual will seek to satisfy the inclination.

A substantial minority of human beings have an instinctive tendency to fulfill same-sex desires. The sex drive itself is innate and instinctive. In most people, this sex drive is directed primarily toward the opposite gender; for still others, their sexual attractions are strong in intensity and frequency primarily toward their own gender. As a conservative estimate, approximately 10% of the U.S. population is predominantly or exclusively homosexual in orientation and behavior (Kinsey, 1948; Kinsey, 1953).

Until the early 1970s, thousands of lesbian and gay persons

sought out psychiatrists and other therapists to help them change their same-sex feelings. Unfortunately, thousands of these individuals wasted their time and money. Most experts now believe that a change in orientation, i.e., in desire and attraction, is not possible.

The helping professions have failed in their long attempt to reverse sexual behavior in lesbian and gay people. For example, Masters and Johnson presented only one actual case of reversion or conversion to heterosexual functioning among 54 male subjects, and this individual was identified as bisexual at the outset (Gramick and Nugent, 1979). In another study of 106 homosexual men, only 29 became exclusively heterosexual in behavior and this change was not known to have lasted beyond two years (Bieber, 1962). More than half of these men were initially bisexual and most of the subjects required 350 or more hours of therapy. Thus, even with a high degree of motivation, an expenditure of much time and money, and an existing predisposition to bisexuality, the possibility of actually altering behavior is extremely low, costly, time consuming, and short lived.

These reports concern alteration of sexual behavior. There is no documentation of permanent alteration of same-sex feelings, attractions, and desires. If it is apparently impossible to modify a homosexual orientation, then these same-sex feelings must be deeply ingrained in the person's psychological makeup. Psychologist Frank A. Beach once claimed, "Various social goals and ethical laws are violated by the homosexual individual, but to describe [such] behavior as 'unnatural' is to depart from strict accuracy" (Churchill, 1967, p. 69).

Although same-sex genital behavior may be the natural psychological result of same-sex love and attractions, strong social sanctions imposed in many cultures frequently inhibit such innate responses to same-sex stimuli and condition people to respond to heterosexual stimuli. Despite strong social taboos, countless individuals persist in expressing these desires and feelings of love for their own gender. If, as some would claim, only heterosexuality is psychologically natural, i.e., instinctively imprinted within an individual's personality structure, how can heterosexuality be obliterated or obscured in millions and millions of people? If, then, "natural" is defined as that which is instinctively and freely experienced without external coercion, same-sex feelings and attractions do indeed seem to be quite natural for a significant proportion of the human population.

Biology

A third definition of natural is illustrated in such phrases as "laws of nature," "naturalist," and "natural history." What is congruent or consistent with the "laws of nature" is deemed natural. This approach to the concept "natural" involves a study of non-living phenomena, plants, and animals. From this perspective, a given characteristic is "natural" for human beings if it is in accordance with their animal heritage.

What is needed here is an application of animal data to human behavior. In research on the sexual behavior of species other than the human, homosexual activity appears frequently in infrahuman primates, such as apes, monkeys, and baboons, especially as they approach adulthood, although this may not be exclusive in many cases. Only recently have scientific studies been conducted to observe same-sex behavior among sub-primate mammals. These studies indicate that homosexual behavior appears in lower mammals, frequently among domestic stock such as sheep, cattle, horses, pigs, and rabbits (Ford and Beach, 1951).

Examples of homosexuality have been found even among the nonmammalian species. Any two male or female pigeons will engage in same-sex behavior when placed together. Phylogenetic data indicate that same-sex behavior becomes both more common and more complex as one ascends the evolutionary scale. Innate homosexual behavior patterns are not exclusively human phenomena but are definitely consonant with the human's mammalian background. As such, they are natural in the biological sense.

Theology

A fourth meaning for the term "natural" is often given by religious persons, primarily in discussions about sexuality. Traditional religious arguments maintain that there are necessary links between marriage and sexual intercourse and between intercourse and biological generation. The classical explanation hinges on the Stoic exultation of natural law. Between the fifteenth and nineteenth centuries, most theologians writing on sexuality divided sexual sins into two categories: those in accordance with nature (i.e., open to procreation) and those contrary to nature (i.e., inhibiting procreation). Thus anal and oral intercourse, masturbation, coitus interruptus, and intercourse during pregnancy were considered sinful, and unnatural. Rape was sinful but natural.

Religious adherents usually refer to biology, often in contradictory ways, to substantiate their arguments. At times the term natural was equated with animal behavior, when, for example, Thomas Aquinas considered contraception "against nature" because beasts look for offspring. Yet, at other times, nature was described as what was different from animals, when, for example, the position in human intercourse of the woman beneath the man was thought to be natural because any other position was comparable to brute animals. Like the early Church Fathers, the scholastic theologians selectively chose their analogies of what was natural in order to reinforce views already held.

Frequently the theological argument is accompanied by explanations regarding the physiological purpose or function of bodily parts. A functional argument goes something like this: God intends that the necessary purpose of the sexual organs is reproduction. Since homosexual activity cannot result in procreation, such acts are contrary to God's intent and are thus unnatural.

The hidden assumption of human ability to know divine intent with certitude can certainly be challenged. How can humans know God's will with moral certainty and without reference to reason and logic? When appeals are made to divine revelation, who decides and interprets revelation?

An obvious function of the genital organs is reproduction. But to maintain that a particular bodily organ serves only one purpose or must serve a certain specified purpose seems provincial at best. In the human evolutionary development, hands serve as a means of grasping, not of walking. Yet who would object that hands be used in conveying greetings or other messages with emotional content because such actions are contrary to the nature of hands? Would anyone deny that the mouth, whose primary purpose is food ingestion, has another and socially more aesthetic function of verbal communication?

If other parts of the body may serve multiple purposes, why is it that the sexual parts may not? To claim, as some have, that the sexual parts are not morally equal to other parts of the body and are of special value because they involve the generation of life betrays a lack of appreciation for other bodily parts and systems, all of which contribute to life. Placing a hierarchy of value on bodily parts leads to an idolatry or sacralization of some parts. Would proponents of a theology that maintains that there is a single or special purpose of bodily parts refuse to admit that another function of the penis is the elimination of urine?

Many moral theologians today acknowledge more than one purpose of human intercourse (Cahill, 1985a; Curran, 1983; Farley, 1983; Guindon, 1986; Keane, 1977; Kosnik, 1977; Maguire, 1983;

McCormick, 1989; McNeill, 1976). They differentiate between the reproductive and unitive functions of sexual intercourse and maintain that the two functions need not be present simultaneously in every genital act in order to render the action ethically responsible. In fact, they point out that concern about the modern world's population explosion and about a reasonable care and stewardship of the earth's resources challenges traditional notions of the meaning of sexuality. They thus liberate God from being controlled by a rigid and predetermined view of reality. A similar theological case is often made by appealing to the structure of the human body: God intends heterosexuality because the male and female parts "fit." Because the vagina is an obvious receptacle for the penis, any use of the male sexual organ other than for the deposit of semen in the vagina is believed to be unnatural. An examination of the male and female bodies, in which the parts manifestly "fit," shows this to be true. But such reasoning is an argument by limitation or restriction. The fact that one form of linkage is obvious and common does not render alternative ways "unnatural." Because human genitals fit together in one way does not preclude other ways of sexual union.

Underlying these philosophical and theological approaches is a definition of nature as that which makes an object what it essentially or actually is or what God intends it to be. The key question, of course, is "What is the divine purpose?" Do such arguments merely interpret human preferences and prejudice as God's will?

Along with divine intent, we must also examine human motives to determine whether insistence on the unnaturalness of homosexuality, or even other sexual acts, is merely a reflection of an unconscious desire to legitimate the existing social order. Unfortunately, the expression of same-sex feelings and desires is often perceived as some kind of threat to the heterosexual structure. Unexamined cultural assumptions influence human perceptions and judgments; what is conveniently regarded as natural is often an expression of deep-seated cultural bias. Appeals to God's intent are at least questionable and can lead to such absurd deductions as "If God wanted human beings to fly, God would have given them wings. So, the airplane is unnatural." While the faith of those who hold these positions cannot be questioned, their interpretation of human sexuality and divine intent regarding sexual expression certainly can and should be.

Contemporary Views

A current understanding of nature is one that is dynamic and constantly in flux. Aristotle taught that fire by its nature moved away from the center of the universe. When science demonstrated the Copernican theory in which the earth was no longer viewed as the central planetary body, the Aristotelian concept of the nature of fire was revised. Similarly, the ancient Greeks believed that every earthly object was composed of earth, air, water, or fire. But a deeper understanding of physics and chemistry demanded a more sophisticated explanation of the nature of any object in the universe. As species of living objects themselves are gradually being transformed by evolution, the human perception of such objects' nature is constantly adapting and in need of revision. Even slight variations in successive generations of a species influence the developing understanding of nature.

Unless rigid or static, a construct of human nature that was popular 500 B.C.E. or 1300 C.E. need not be identical to a contemporary perception of human nature. We continually incorporate scientific advancement and current data from the behavioral sciences to revise our understanding of human nature. Accurate knowledge regarding human reproduction was not discovered until after 1875. Basing their philosophical and theological arguments in the context of the biology of their day, religious leaders of the past cannot be faulted for a limited analysis of human sexuality. With the quantum leaps that have been achieved in biology, psychology, and sociology, minds in the twentieth and twenty-first centuries must subject traditional religious arguments about nature to more thorough and critical analyses. Today's personalist interpretation of human nature is not bound by a static view reminiscent of Freud's "biology is destiny" but rather is struggling to free itself from biological imperatives.

Conclusion

When all the debate is over about what is natural and what is unnatural about human sexuality, what many people, perhaps subconsciously, mean is that same-sex attraction is not experienced by the majority of people. This may be the case because Kinsey's figures indicate that slightly more than half of the population is exclusively heterosexual in feelings and behaviors; i.e., they do not experience even slight or incidental same-sex attractions or fantasies. But the Kinsey figures may be somewhat higher than reality on the heterosexual side because Kinsey's data were collected at a time when people were less willing to acknowledge their same-sex feelings. Current researchers are finding slight increases in the proportions of homosexual acknowledgments.

If North American society tolerated a gay or lesbian lifestyle, the incidence of homosexuality might become more visible. It is unlikely that there would be mass conversions of heterosexuals to homosexuality. Rather, people would feel freer to express the homosexual or bisexual feelings they already have. In societies that condone homosexual behavior, a heterosexual lifestyle is still preponderant. We can reasonably be assured that a homosexual lifestyle would not become the norm.

The majority can, and often does, reveal its prejudice and intolerance for diversity. Because the majority of individuals feel, react, or believe one way, must all persons do so? As long as the minority group does not harm or infringe on the majority and vice-versa, the two should be able to co-exist peacefully. The sociologist Becker (1963), who has written considerably about the societal outsider, states, "Social groups create deviance by making the rules whose infraction constitutes deviance, and by applying those rules to particular people and labelling them as outsiders" (p. 9).

I harbor a cherished hope that all peoples in the human family may live together as true brothers and sisters. Only when the majority in each culture accords respect for the rights and dignity of the racial, ethnic, sexual, economic, and religious minorities in its midst can we hope to have a truly free and just society. Only when our unspoken fears and insecurities are recognized and our unnamed ignorance and biases erased, can we work collaboratively in realizing the fullness of the exciting human project upon the earth.

PART TWO

COUNSELING AND PASTORAL ISSUES

4. Gay Sons and Lesbian Daughters
Robert Nugent

5. Lesbian Women and the Church
Jeannine Gramick

6. Married and Gay, Married and Lesbian
Robert Nugent

–4–

Gay Sons
and Lesbian Daughters

I knew why they came to my apartment for coun-
seling, but it took them a long time to say it. They were a Catholic
couple in their mid-40's, parents of two children, both Catholic
college graduates, both professionals in a small suburban area.
Their younger child, a boy, was still in high school and their
daughter was a sophomore in a small Middle Western college.
They had just returned from a Christmas meeting with the daughter in Chicago. She took them out to dinner to a nice restaurant,
and she had a drink or two before dinner. Then she told them.
The mother became physically ill and had to leave the table.

They both shifted nervously on the couch, their eyes down, as they came closer to telling me. Finally, the father, filling up with tears as he spoke, said softly, guiltily, "Our daughter is a homosexual." The mother was crying too. So we sat quietly for a few moments. Then we began to talk about how they felt about what they now knew, what it really meant to them and to the family, and how they were going to cope with it.

It was not an unusual counseling session for me. Since the early seventies I have been through similar scenes with countless parents. This couple was fortunate. They had someone to talk to about the situation. They could ask some basic questions, and I promised them some good reading materials. I might see them again, or I might not. Sometimes all such people need is a start on the road to discovery and eventual acceptance.

There are many parents who will not or cannot bring themselves to tell someone about a homosexual son or daughter. Whether they suspect it, or have discovered it accidentally, or the child has shared it with them, their confusion and pain finds no healing ministry. Their questions go unanswered. Their fears go unallayed. "What will the pastor think of us as parents?" "What will the rest of the family think when they find out?"

Many parents of gay sons or lesbian daughters will not approach the parish priest with the problem because "he's a close friend of the family" or simply because they are too ashamed or embarrassed to talk about it. Sometimes when parents get up the courage to go to the priest, they get the sense that he is just as uncomfortable talking about it as they are, or that the whole situation is as surprising and confusing or upsetting to him as it is to them.

Homosexuality in the family is an emerging issue in the church of the 1990s. Like so many other sensitive and controversial questions facing the church today, homosexuality is an issue that arouses strong feelings on all sides of the question. Unlike many of the other issues, however, it is also one of those family-related problems that most people are reluctant to talk about, let alone admit they are dealing with in their own family. We treat lesbian and gay members of our family in much the same way we treated alcoholics years ago: We don't let anyone else know about them. I do not believe that the comparison to alcoholism is valid, but I do know that parental reactions to the two issues are sometimes similar. Some people do not want anyone to know about a gay or lesbian person in the family. Some parents are too frightened to even imagine that one of their own children might possibly be homosexually oriented.

Family Ministry

In the U.S. Catholic bishops' plan of pastoral action for family ministry, *A Vision and Strategy*, published in 1978, the bishops showed an awareness of the problem when they spoke of a ministry to "hurting families." Among "hurting families" they listed families dealing with poverty, aging, alcoholism, drug abuse, and homosexuality. In 1976 the American bishops had already called for a "special degree of pastoral understanding and care" for homosexual persons. In the family-ministry document, the bishops also noted the complexities of the issues involved in "hurting families." They stated that not every parish priest or pastoral counselor is necessarily competent to deal with alcoholism, drug abuse, or homosexuality. "Clergy and couples engaged in family ministry," the plan says, "should be encouraged and helped to acquire specialized skills for dealing with such complex issues" as those listed above.

As the church continues to evolve its understanding and expand its practice of ministry, I foresee a specialized ministry developing among those who have acquired a certain pastoral expertise in the area of homosexuality and who are able to support and minister to families coping with homosexuality. I have in mind especially the possibility of peer ministry by parents who have already gone through the experience of dealing with homosexuality in the family, and who would be willing to help other parents in what is always a traumatic experience. After more than twenty years of working in this area, I have no doubt that there is a quiet but pressing need for such a ministry.

In the Catholic community the issue of how homosexuality affects parents was first addressed in the late seventies. Two nationally known Catholic experts in family ministry, both syndicated writers, devoted full columns to the topic in the Catholic press. Dr. James Kenny in an article entitled "Our Only Son Is a Homosexual" gave sensitive and sound advice to parents wondering if they should reveal a son's homosexuality to his sister. And Dolores Curran in "Homosexuality and the Catholic Parent," responding to a letter from a mother whose daughter had come "under the influence of a lesbian," admitted frankly, "I don't know how to respond." I think the latter feeling is a common one among Catholic parents.

The first obstacle in getting a handle on the subject has to do with the fact that the evidence from the empirical sciences of anthropology, sociology, cross cultural studies, human sexuality studies, psychology, and psychiatry is often contradictory. Hardly any other contemporary topic contains so little definite information or so few particular points of unanimous agreement among the experts. There are, for example, a variety of viewpoints on how to define homosexuality, who is a homosexual, how a homosexual orientation arises, and what are the realistic chances of changing a person's sexual orientation once it has become fairly well established as part of the individual's psychosexual identity and status.

Although the American Psychiatric Association no longer officially classifies homosexuality as a mental illness, some psychiatrists and psychologists still consider homosexuality some form of maladjustment or at least a manifestation of a personality disorder, however minimal. Claims of success in changing or reversing homosexuality, such as those of Masters and Johnson, when investigated thoroughly, always turn out to be cases of altering only one's sexual behavior or helping a person function physically with a member of the other sex. Sometimes the means to accomplish this, however, raise more serious moral questions than does the original homosexual behavior.

In our American culture and society, homosexuality is a very emotional topic often associated, or confused, with related but distinct issues of masculinity or femininity. Given our traditional American Christian views and feelings about human sexuality and what we consider normal, it is a threatening experience for most males to face the fact that a son is homosexually oriented. Mothers, it seems, are generally better able to respond personally to homosexual children, male or female, than are fathers. Mothers are also generally better able to appreciate the emotional, affective, or romantic components of a true homosexual orientation than are fathers or men who see homosexuality only in terms of same-sex behavior rather than love and commitment.

There are some commentators who claim that the strong negative emotions evoked by gay or lesbian people are directly related to the fact that most people have had some feelings or experiences of homosexuality in their own lives but are afraid to deal with them. Homophobia is a term that has been coined to describe an irrational fear or hatred of homosexual feelings in oneself or in others. It is surely evident that our society has carefully spelled out expectations about how men and women should act, respond, and react to each other. Appearance, mannerisms, behavior, and interests that are not congruent with one's gender are inaccurately and unfortunately labeled homosexual and, as a result, everyone suffers.

We often confuse sexual orientation with gender role; the latter is a cultural expectation of what it means to be masculine or feminine. We then run the risk of causing serious problems for children in our families who do not fit the "all-American male" stereotype or the "beauty queen female" model but who are definitely not homosexually oriented. There are even some theorists who say that if parents insist on trying to force male children, for instance, into conforming to masculine stereotypes of being tough, athletic, or independent, we might inadvertently be contributing to the formation of a homosexual identity in the child. Ideally, we ought to help children develop and grow comfortable with those individual qualities, personal traits, and unique capabilities that are basically human without having to label them or the children "masculine" or "feminine."

Parents should be aware that homosexual behavior, especially in the early prepubescent and adolescent years, does not necessarily indicate a homosexual orientation. Homosexual activity can come about from a number of factors and kinds of motivations, including curiosity, experimentation, temporary anxiety about relating to the opposite sex, or even as part of a search for sexual identity. In some few cases, homosexual activity and association can be used as a sign of rebellion to get back at parents, to embrace a popular cause such as gay rights, or to fill a need for group acceptance. This is usually called temporary or situational homosexuality and does not last if the person is not homosexually oriented.

There are, however, individuals who are truly and definitely homosexually oriented and, in many cases, are aware of that orientation from their early years. Men in our society generally come to an awareness of their homosexuality primarily from its physical manifestations and at an earlier age than women. Many gay men speak in counseling of having had an awareness they were different even at the age of nine or ten, although they might not have known at that time what homosexuality actually was. If this is the case, then it is not as likely, as some parents want to believe, that a child's homosexuality is "just a stage that they are passing through."

It is not my purpose in this chapter to discuss theories about the genesis of a homosexual or heterosexual orientation, or how parents might "prevent" a child from developing a homosexual identity, if indeed that is possible. John Money (1986) from Johns Hopkins gender-identity clinic in Baltimore believes that, from a combination of prenatal and postnatal factors, gender identity and sexual orientation are firmly established by the age of three when language skills are formed. Just as a child is born with the biological or physical capacity to speak, but has to learn how to speak a native or fundamental language, most theorists believe that there is both a biological and an environmental component of homosexuality. John Money emphasizes the importance of the biological components; other sexual researchers place more emphasis on the critical period of adolescence and its sexual-identity crisis.

A healthy family environment with strong role models, honest communication, loving relationships, and a general comfortableness with human sexuality and the body have been seen as the optimal environment for, and predictor of, heterosexual orientation. Yet at the same time, studies indicate individuals who come from this kind of family environment can be homosexually oriented. The nature/nurture debate about the origin of a homosexual orientation continues among professionals today.

What about those individuals who are homosexually oriented? What happens in the family when they decide to share this awareness with parents and siblings? How can church ministry help parents in this kind of situation? From my own counseling experience, I have formulated several common responses that might help parents deal with homosexually-oriented children.

Common Responses

The gradual discovery of one's homosexual orientation involves a deep and constant sense of being different from everybody else and, at the same time, a tremendous amount of pressure to keep that difference hidden from others. Along with this goes a certain amount of guilt, a lot of fear, and much confusion. Not being able to share this with those who are closest to us means that a person must live with a sense of isolation and loneliness that non-gay people may not understand or cannot imagine. When a child of any age chooses to share the orientation with a parent, the parent should realize the external and internal pressures under which the child has lived for so many years and the effects on his or her sense of value and self-esteem.

Sharing one's homosexual orientation with a parent is an act of trust on the part of the child. I know gay and lesbian people who have told everyone in their lives about their orientation except their parents. Either they think the parents "just couldn't handle it," or else they do not want to cause them any unnecessary pain. And yet I think that most homosexual people want to share that part of who they are with their parents, especially when the levels of communication in a family have been deep, open, and honest. Telling one's parents is a tremendous risk for the gay son or lesbian daughter, but a risk that most are willing to take when the time is right. Sometimes the parents can help make the time right.

It is helpful if the parent indicates somehow that it is all right to bring up the topic either personally or in terms of a magazine article, film, or television program that both have seen. This can serve as a gentle introduction to the topic and as a lead into self-disclosure. It can prevent the shock approach that usually comes in a letter. "Dear Mom and Dad: I have wanted to tell you for many years that I am gay..." It can prevent the shock that comes by way of information from friends or through an accidental discovery. This openness prevents the common situation of a mutual and unspoken agreement not to talk about it. "I'm sure they know I'm gay, but they just don't want to talk about it."

Parents ought to be aware that it is not unusual for their reactions to their son's or daughter's disclosure to parallel in some degree the stages of dying that have received so much attention in the past years. Parents go through similar stages in coming to grips with a child's homosexuality or lifestyle. These stages include shock and anger ("Why does this happen to our family?"), denial ("It's only a stage she's going through"), bargaining ("We'll get him the best psychiatrist"), depression ("We'd rather not see you or talk about it"), and acceptance ("She's my daughter and I love her and we'll work things out somehow.") Depending on the availability of outside help and counseling, these various stages last longer in some instances than in others. Many parents need some kind of ministry, preferably a church-related one, that can help them sort out and evaluate their feelings and the decisions they are forced to make.

In learning to cope with this new piece of information and the impact it will have, for better or worse, on the parent-child relationship, both parents and the child need to realize and appreciate the necessity of open, honest dialogue and on-going discussion of the issue. Some homosexual people expect, and at times even demand, that parents accept them fully and immediately in everything they say or do. They do not even afford their parents opportunities to talk about their legitimate fears and concerns or to give voice to the many questions they naturally may have. These are issues that may impact greatly on the life of a person they know and love. Some lesbian and gay people feel that parental questions are really signs of disapproval, even after their parents have expressed a desire to understand and accept the child.

On the other hand, some parents refuse to listen to their child's feelings and experiences about being homosexual or to show any interest in their lives once they have discovered their orientation. Some parents, while trying to understand, are reluctant to ask questions out of fear that their questions and interest might be interpreted as rejection. The usual amount of pain is compounded when there is not a sufficient amount of trust, patience, and understanding on both sides.

If gay and lesbian people ask that parents, peers, and siblings try to understand them, they also have a corresponding responsibility. They need to provide others with the information and time to assimilate the new knowledge, to get in touch with their real feelings, and to express them honestly. This will help initiate and continue a dialogue where people can grow in mutual understanding of the other's perspectives. If there is any instant labeling or judging on either side of the family, then chances for an acceptable, liveable, and healthy solution are almost nil. Where there has been slow growth, mutual trust, and love, the experience has bound families more closely together.

Invariably one of the issues that arises in discussions on homosexuality is the question of morality. From a Catholic viewpoint there is no lack of clarity concerning the church's position. A homosexual orientation is morally neutral. Lesbian and gay individuals are no more responsible for their homosexual orientation than are heterosexual people for theirs. One Roman Catholic bishop has compared a homosexual orientation with being left-handed. On the other hand, homosexual behavior as distinct from orientation is morally unacceptable either because it involves use of genital sexuality that lacks a necessary component of male-female procreative potential or because it is sexual activity outside the bonds of marriage. Confessors are advised in official church documents to treat people with compassion and understanding while allowing for various factors such as habit, erroneous conscience, and compulsion that might lessen personal responsibility and culpability for homosexual activity.

The present pastoral ministry of the church requires gay and lesbian people to live in chaste celibacy with the help of the sacraments, spiritual direction, and works of charity. A growing number of reputable theologians allow, on the pastoral level, for the formation of stable, faithful homosexual relationships. These relationships would embody some of the traditional values associated with heterosexual marriages such as fidelity, monogamy, and permanence. Referring to such relationships, the Catholic bishops of England and Wales stated that, while the moral norms were clear, when we help people apply their consciences to such situations as stable relationships, the clear-cut application of such moral norms may be complicated.

Parents often ask, "How can I accept my gay son or lesbian daughter, whom I love, without accepting his or her lifestyle?" Priests hear similar questions in reference to a child who has married outside the church. While it might be easy to say we have to "love the sinner but hate the sin," it is always more difficult to make that distinction in practice. A homosexual orientation is in no way sinful, and we are wrong to make any judgments about a person simply because we know he or she is homosexually oriented. There are many celibate gay or lesbian persons. Nor is all homosexual activity subjectively sinful for all people at all times as the Vatican *Declaration on Sexual Ethics* affirms when it talks about those factors that might lessen responsibility. The moral evaluation of homosexual activity can be as complex as the psychological and social evaluation. The Catholic bishops from the

State of Washington, for example, have said that "even with regard to homogenital activity no one except Almighty God can make certain judgments about the personal sinfulness of acts" (Washington State Catholic Conference, 1983, p. 4).

There are many other issues to be discussed, such as how parents should react when a son or daughter is involved in a relationship with another gay or lesbian person, or whether they should let their child bring the "friend" into the house, or whether they should visit the couple if they are living together. Parents are also genuinely concerned about whether or how to tell younger children in the family. With judicious reading, counseling from competent people, and a whole lot of trust, the situation need not be tragic for anyone, nor need it split a family into embittered groups.

In dealing with homosexuality we are often facing our own ignorance of facts, our fears, myths, and stereotypes about sexuality and homosexuality, and a long history and tradition of harsh attitudes. We are confronting the pain and the isolation of many of our children who are gay or lesbian. We are dealing with alienated Catholics who have much in common with divorced and remarried Catholics in their feelings that the church has rejected them. This is a challenging ministry for the church as it works to build strong, loving families based on justice, compassion, and dignity for all people.

We are just beginning, slowly and cautiously, to move into this ministry, which is so new and so threatening. We are beginning to realize that lesbian and gay people are, always have been, and always will be part of our families. We should make our own the words of the Commission for the Plan of Pastoral Action for Family Ministry (1979) of the Archdiocese of Milwaukee. It says,

While recognizing the value of the nuclear family, the reality of present society has necessitated the broadening of our concept and practice of family ministry to acknowledge other lifestyles including, but not necessarily limited to, single parent families, childless couples, the widowed, the separated, sexual minorities....It is our prayer that...all people will come to see the Church as the caring and loving community it is meant to be. It is our wish that the unchurched and the lukewarm will see in our efforts a genuine desire to unite once again in the true spirit of Christian unity. It is our deep desire that parents and singles, divorced and widowed, the young and the aged, the heterosexual and the homosexual...will find in the Family of God the love, the encouragement, the acceptance and the hope we all need to live productive and fulfilling lives (pp. 1, 6).

–5–

Lesbian Women
and the Church

For the first few years of my involvement in lesbian and gay ministry, most of my association was with gay men. As my ministry grew, I came to know more and more lesbian women. I remember feeling disturbed with a lesbian couple who seemed perpetually angry and bitter. Yet I liked very much a young, pleasant, intelligent lesbian activist who worked with the American Civil Liberties Union. I worked closely with a sensible and attractive former nun to establish the Baltimore chapter of Dignity, a support group for lesbian and gay Catholics. I felt the goodness of a lesbian couple who eventually founded the Conference for Catholic Lesbians because of an idea born at a retreat I co-conducted for lesbian women. I came to appreciate that lesbian women are as different in personalities and in talents as heterosexual women. My old stereotype that lesbian and gay persons were psychologically maladjusted was destroyed by personal encounters with women who were generally caring, responsible, and common-sensed contributors to society.

Extreme, Subtle, and Personal Homophobia

From lesbian women I learned much about society's homophobia and negative judgments about homosexuality. Societal attitudes toward lesbianism are marked by widespread, almost universal intolerance. I learned that homophobia can be extreme, it can be subtle, and it can be very personal.

If women have felt marginalized, ignored, or unempowered in social and ecclesial milieus, lesbian women, relegated to the lowest rung of the power-elite ladder, feel the oppression in multiple measure. One of the largest minorities, lesbian women across the globe number upwards of 140 million, more than nine times the number of world Jews. Lesbian women are often subjected to unjust and outright discrimination, mental abuse, and even physical violence.

Lesbian women have been sentenced to many years of hard labor in Pakistan and the Soviet Union and forced into mental institutions in China. An Argentinian woman's social position is jeopardized by a public disclosure of lesbianism. In Iran, lesbian and gay people have been executed. Almost everywhere lesbian women, if open about their orientation, fear for their lives and their livelihood. Necessary secrecy and enforced invisibility rob lesbian women of their human, God-given dignity. They are forced to maintain a heterosexual charade.

In progressive Norway, a lesbian member of the Norwegian Parliament endured a sophisticated but unsuccessful five-month

campaign against her renomination to the Norwegian Conservative Party by "Christians" who publicly claimed, "Lesbians and
gays be cursed." The City Council of Wellington, New Zealand,
refused to display a bus advertisement that read, "Lesbians, contact your local community." In Mozambique, lesbian women are
sent to rehabilitation camps to learn the "correct" orientation. In a
1980 United Nations Human Rights Commission meeting in Ge-
neva, the Netherlands accused the United States of showing an
alarming lack of tolerance by not granting entrance visas to lesbian women and gay men.

The U.S. has done little to protect the personal liberties of its
lesbian citizens. As publicity increases surrounding the spread of
AIDS and as advocacy for lesbian and gay civil rights becomes
more vocal and more visible, anti-homosexual backlash has dramatically intensified. An annual study by the National Gay and
Lesbian Task Force since 1984 concluded that violence against lesbian women is widespread. Approximately one in ten lesbians
has been punched, kicked, or beaten. Slightly more than that ratio
have suffered police harassment; 40% reported sexual assault.
Overall, nine in ten women experience some form of victimization
simply for being lesbian or for being perceived as lesbian.

From lesbian women I learned that homophobia can be subtly
as well as blatantly manifested. Discrimination in employment,
for example, can be motivated by homophobia but masked in the
guise of happenstance. I have met a number of lesbian women
who said that their positions at work were eliminated when their
employers learned of their lesbianism, although this reason was
never mentioned.

In the late 1970s, I conducted a study about the coming out process and coping strategies of lesbian women. In this study, I
found that, because of co-workers' suspicions of lesbianism, 23%
of the sample had employment related problems including job

termination or promotional failures. Half of the women knew other lesbians who experienced similar work problems. Most lesbian women would feel more secure if federal civil rights legislation existed to protect them from job termination. Although such legislation, supported by a majority of the U.S. public, would not totally eliminate work discrimination, lesbian women and gay men would at least possess legal recourse. However, to date, no such legislation exists on a federal level.

Statistics fail to convey the overwhelming anger, intense pain, and well-founded fear experienced by these victims. An anthology by Zanotti (1986) provides compelling personal accounts of the oppression Catholic lesbian women experience. Other literature (Gramick, 1983) also contains valuable personal reports by lesbians as well as theoretical reflections.

For example, in 1981 a young woman was maced and abducted near her apartment, mentally abused, and sexually assaulted repeatedly for one week because her parents had hired men to "deprogram" their daughter from a life of lesbianism. These parents believed that physical force was justified to "save" their daughter. Our churches had not prepared these parents to accept and to love their lesbian daughter as a gift and child of God. In a Massachusetts town with a sizable lesbian community, several lesbians were physically and sexually molested, and lesbian establishments were vandalized.

These are not isolated instances of homophobia in action. According to several municipal surveys, approximately 90% of anti-lesbian crimes are not reported to governmental authorities. Lesbian women are discouraged from prosecuting because they fear legal sanctions and even further victimization from the authorities themselves.

A 1981 report on "Discrimination Against Homosexuals" was accepted by the Parliamentary Assembly of the Council of Europe. Composed of representatives of 21 European countries, the Assembly acts as a weather vane to express as well as to shape public opinion. One of the recommendations advocated equal treatment for lesbian and gay persons in employment, salary and job security, and a change in law in those member states in which private same-sex acts between consenting adults are subject to criminal prosecution. This marked the first time that any international body recognized lesbian and gay rights as a human rights issue. Amnesty International works for the release of anyone imprisoned for sexual orientation or for advocating lesbian and gay rights. It has never discriminated because of sexual orientation.

From lesbian women I also learned that homophobia can be rooted in personal fears and anxieties about one's own sexuality. More and more we are beginning to realize that same-sex erotic feelings, even though not predominant in most individuals, are quite natural. But unless we make friends with our own homosexual passions, we will be imprisoned by them. Repressed feelings, which we consider unacceptable, invariably erupt in unhealthy ways, destructive of self or others.

Church Response

How has the Catholic church responded to the social discrimination against lesbian women? According to recent polls, a majority of U.S. Catholics support equal job opportunities for lesbian women and gay men and also advocate legalizing homosexual acts between consenting adults in private. This is quite hopeful, since it indicates that a majority of grassroots Catholics have positive attitudes regarding legal rights for lesbian and gay persons. Most surprising of all, approximately one-third believe that homosexual behavior is not necessarily sinful and that homosexualty is a valid alternative lifestyle (Gallup and Castelli, 1987; Chandler, 1987; Teichner, 1989). Because dissent is more widespread among younger Catholics where 39% under the age of 40 disagree with the traditional teaching on homogenital behavior, the percentage will likely increase in the future (Chandler, 1987).

Lesbian and gay Catholics have responded by organizing. In the United States the national organization, Dignity, grew to a strength of 5000 members by the mid-seventies. A group of lesbian women in Dignity, dissatisfied with the male predominance of the group, formed the Conference for Catholic Lesbians in 1983. Catholic groups in other countries were also formed; their significance is discussed in Chapter 12. By 1986, 58 gay Christian groups in 12 European countries had organized into a forum for faith development and for acceptance of same-sex lifestyles; a number of these groups are primarily Catholic.

Beginning in the 1970s, an increasing number of Catholic institutions, national organizations, and religious orders began to speak out on behalf of social justice and civil rights for lesbian and gay people (Nugent and Gramick, 1982). In 1974, the National Coalition of American Nuns became the first national Catholic organization to pass a resolution stating that discrimination based on sexual orientation was immoral and should be illegal. Subsequently, the National Federation of Priests' Councils, the National Assembly of Religious Brothers, and the National Assembly of Women Religious made similar public statements. The Quixote Center was the first Catholic social justice center to take up the cause of lesbian and gay rights.

It is significant that a number of mainstream Catholic groups reached out to lesbian and gay organizations or to those ministering to and with them. The United States Catholic Conference invited Dignity to send a representative to the 1976 "Call to Action" Conference in Detroit, which was the official celebration of the U.S. bicentennial by the National Conference of Catholic Bishops. The resolutions passed there by more than 3000 delegates helped to place lesbian and gay concerns on the agenda of many dioceses and organizations. Many religious congregations and some bishops provided moral and financial support to New Ways Ministry, a Catholic group that Bob Nugent and I co-founded in 1977 to serve as a reconciling bridge between the lesbian and gay community and the official church. In the mid-1980s the Conference for Catholic Lesbians was invited to join the Women-Church Convergence, a coalition of progressive Catholic women's groups. All of these initiatives and many more indicated that the U.S. Catholic community was becoming more aware and more accepting of lesbian and gay people.

On official church levels, there have also been attempts to uphold the human rights of lesbian and gay persons and to be sensitive to their life experiences. The Catholic Social Welfare Commission (1981) of the Bishops of England and Wales published a booklet that acknowledged that lesbianism differs substantially from male homosexuality. This was evidence that Bishop Augustine Harris's writing committee met with representatives of the Catholic Lesbian Sisterhood to listen to their personal experience. The Catholic Lesbian Sisterhood publicly welcomed the guidelines.

As early as 1976, the National Conference of Catholic Bishops (1976) stated in their pastoral letter on moral values that "homosexuals should not suffer from prejudice against their basic human rights. They have a right to respect, friendship and justice and should have an active role in the Christian community" (p. 19). Ten years later, the Congregation for the Doctrine of the Faith (1986) voiced words of support for lesbian and gay civil rights when it said, "The intrinsic dignity of each person must always be respected in word, in action, and in law" (par. 10).

Individual bishops, as well as bishops' conferences, have publicly spoken against homophobia and violence toward lesbian and gay persons. The Washington State Catholic Conference (1983) published a document outlining church teaching about the evils of prejudice against lesbian and gay persons. Because church people have contributed to fostering anti-gay prejudice, the document says that the church is seriously obliged to work toward the elimination of this great moral evil. The Congregation for the Doctrine of the Faith (1986) reaffirmed that "it is deplorable that homosexual persons have been and are the object of violent malice in speech and in action" (par. 10). Most recently, the U.S. bishops, at their national meeting in November 1990 called on all Christians of good will to confront homophobic fears, humor, and discrimination.

Nevertheless, all of this Catholic teaching regarding respect and dignity toward lesbian and gay persons is gravely undermined by the actions of some church leaders. The Catholic Council for Church and Society (1980), an agency of the hierarchy of the Netherlands, frankly acknowledged that church pronouncements rejecting social discrimination seriously lack credibility because church actions often contradict church principles. This happens, for example, when Catholic bishops oppose civil rights efforts that embody the teaching of justice for lesbian and gay persons.

Although these official statements note the church's special responsibility to help eliminate injustice, they clearly restate traditional church teaching that homogenital acts are intrinsically immoral. Lesbian women and gay men claim that this teaching itself is discriminatory because it requires lifelong celibacy of homosexual but not of heterosexual persons. They ask instead for realistic guidelines for living a whole and holy sexual life. The Washington State Catholic Conference (1983) document admits that rethinking and development of sexual ethics is needed and the Dutch document points out that the church must find more compelling reasons, if any exist, for rejecting homosexual behavior.

All these efforts toward amelioration, reconciliation, and pastoral outreach to lesbian and gay Catholics were set back at least 20 years by the *Letter to the Bishops of the Catholic Church on the Pastoral Care of Homosexual Persons* from the Congregation for the Doctrine of the Faith (1986). The letter is inappropriately named because most of the 18 paragraphs betray little pastoral concern. Most of the letter is devoted to stemming the tide of increasing acceptance of same-sex behavior. It seemed to devalue individuals it considered threats to the social fabric and implied that individual bishops have been manipulated into supporting a change in civil statutes. Instead of condemning the perpetrators of violence against lesbian women and gay men, the Vatican letter claimed that increasing violence is understandable. In a classic example of blaming the victim, the Congregation erroneously asserted that lesbian and gay people have no "conceivable right" to any civil legislation that protects their behavior. Society, the Congregation said, should not be "surprised" when "violent reactions increase" because of their advocacy for such civil legislation (par. 10). In the U.S., the National Coalition of American Nuns compared the persecution of lesbian and gay Catholics through the Congregation's letter with the Vatican's unjust treatment of Archbishop Raymond Hunthausen and moral theologian Charles Curran.

In discussing the Vatican's letter in a radio interview, Cardinal Adrianus Simonis, the Primate of the Netherlands, contended that a Catholic could refuse to rent an apartment to a lesbian woman or gay man. In addition to stormy criticism from Catholic and Protestant leaders, the 17,000 member Association for the Integration of Homosexuality sued the Cardinal for encouraging discrimination. Although the court ruled in the Cardinal's favor, saying he was entitled to voice the church's teaching on homosexuality, it is questionable whether or not discrimination against lesbian and gay people in housing constitutes part of the church's teaching. Using the same logic, Catholic property owners could then refuse to rent to divorced persons and to married couples who practice artificial means of birth control. But it is unlikely that any church leaders would advocate such a policy.

At the same time Cardinal Simonis was sued by a group of women's rights advocates for encouraging discrimination against women. Writing in a theological journal, the Cardinal stated that feminist theology threatens the priority of man in the order of creation and that the conception process biologically proves woman's inherently passive roles. The Utrecht court dismissed the suit on technical grounds.

Other church actions belie articulated opposition to anti-homosexual and anti-female bias. A nurse's aide at a nun's retirement home in Minnesota was fired summarily when her nun supervisor discovered she was lesbian. Instead of using the publication of the sensational book _Lesbian Nuns: Breaking Silence_ as a teachable moment to discuss a sensitive topic with empathy and compassion, one bishop denounced the anthology as a denigration of religious life; other prelates successfully pressured TV stations to cancel interviews with Curb and Manahan (1985), the book's editors. One contributor was subsequently fired from her position as spiritual director at a Catholic retreat center because of her essay in the book.

Even the progressive international journal _Concilium_ succumbed to theological discrimination against lesbian women. Because of anticipated ecclesiastical pressure, the Italian publisher censored the issue _Women: Invisible in Church and Theology_ by omitting an article that dealt with lesbian experience. Ultimately the Board of _Concilium's_ Foundation apologized to the author, stated that the decision was not a good one, and admitted that it had violated its own policy of non-interference without consultation with the responsible directors.

From a direct analysis of the societal and ecclesial state of the lesbian issue, a number of conclusions emerge:

1. Prejudicial attitudes manifested in concrete acts of discrimination are not limited to society but occur in church structures as well.

2. Generally only lip service is paid to episcopal pronouncements on social justice toward women and lesbian and gay people.

3. Grassroots Catholics appear more favorable than the hierarchy to effecting civil rights for lesbian and gay persons and toward accepting homogenital behavior in loving relationships.

4. Lesbian and gay Catholics have organized to combat the discrimination of invisibility in the church.

5. Lesbian and gay concerns have been placed on the political and pastoral agenda of a number of Catholic organizations.

The fact that church representatives repeatedly treat homosexuality as a male phenomenon is an affront to lesbian women. Their lack of attention to lesbian women is not excused by the possibility that there may be more gay men than lesbian women, but can be more properly explained by the church's unwillingness to take women as seriously as men. Because lesbian women bear the double social disadvantage of being female and homosexual in patriarchal, heterosexist institutions, they must constantly struggle to maintain church allegiance and to challenge their church's persistent blindness to lesbianism. Because lesbian discrimination exists in a matrix of anti-female prejudice of epidemic proportion, it is often difficult to distinguish anti-lesbian bias from anti-woman bias. Both are rooted in misogyny and the preservation of sex-role stereotypes.

Confronting the Sin of Homophobia

Official church response to lesbianism can best be characterized as denial and neglect. Many Catholic bishops simply reiterate that homogenital activity is intrinsically immoral, as if constant denunciations will confirm or compel belief in the hearts of the faithful. Relatively few bishops have confronted the rampant sin of homophobia. Many grassroots Catholics believe that the church is obsessed with sexual bodily parts while lesbian lives are stunted or destroyed. The church should now vigorously attend to the welfare of the whole body of women by opposing intolerance in all its forms. Clergy and laity alike should enter into a dialogue with lesbian women and initiate measures to remedy the exclusion that lesbian and heterosexual women face. Personal and structural attitudes toward women and homosexuality need to be reexamined.

We need a conversion of heart that will take us "back to the basics" of the early Christian community. We may have to choose between "defending church teaching" and proclaiming Jesus' message of love. Our good and gracious God created people who are sexually different from the majority. Can we accept and actively listen to "the other"? Only when the church invites lesbian women to a fuller participation in the church will we imitate the Jesus of the Gospel who welcomed all people into his community of friends.

–6–

Married and Gay, Married and Lesbian

In response to "Homosexuality and the Hurting Family" (Nugent, 1981), one woman wrote, "I would be particularly interested in information and help for married spouses. Specifically, how does a wife handle the awareness that her husband is homosexual? Is she wise in continuing to protect him from her knowledge?" Many others asked similar questions. Not all of them were as dispassionate.

Some spoke from bitter and painful feelings of betrayal and confusion following separation and divorce. In every group of separated and divorced Catholics some individuals tell of their experiences of marital breakups due to homosexuality. Most of them share common feelings of shock and denial when they first learn of their spouse's homosexuality. In some cases the suspicion of homosexuality grows gradually; in others, the awareness was present even before the marriage.

The movie "Making Love" dramatically brought the situation of married gay men to the American filmgoer. It portrayed an apparently happy and successful married professional couple whose marriage ends in divorce after the husband reveals his homosexuality to a wife who insists she can "deal with" anything but silence. Watching and listening to her reactions in several full face monologues, the viewer empathizes with her anger, frustration, and pain. Some viewers may even sympathize with the wife's eventual understanding and acceptance of her husband's new lifestyle, although the neat movie solution is seldom mirrored in real life.

Motivations and Married Gay and Lesbian People

The film raised a host of new questions for many people. Why do some gay and lesbian people marry in the first place? How many married homosexual individuals are there? Can such a relationship really ever work? What about telling family, friends, and relatives? This chapter will attempt to provide some answers to these questions. It will also offer some suggestions for ministering to married lesbian and gay people. Finally, it will discuss ways in which the church can apply preventive medicine to deal with the reality of homosexuality before it reaches the crisis situation requiring the dissolution of a marriage.

It is impossible to determine the exact number of gay men and lesbian women in heterosexual marriages simply because most study samples are not representative. Married homosexual people are obviously much less likely to participate in such surveys in the first place. A study by Weinberg and Williams (1974) reported that gay men who were currently married tended to be the most covert, the most worried about having their homosexuality revealed, and the least integrated into the gay world in comparison with their unmarried counterparts. Other reliable studies have found that approximately 20% of gay men, and an even higher percentage of lesbian women, have been married at least once during their lives to a heterosexual partner. Although we can never know exactly how many married homosexual people there are in the population, the literature indicates that such marriages, while not commonplace, are not extremely unusual.

Counseling experiences and studies indicate that greater proportions of lesbian women enter into heterosexual unions than gay males. One reason is that women come to an awareness of their sexuality and, in the cases of homosexual women, acceptance of it later in their lives than do men. In many cases this means after a heterosexual marriage has been contracted. Societal pressures to find their identity, security, and social role in marriage and family influence lesbian women no less than other women.

Gay men and lesbian women marry for a variety of reasons. In many instances, they are simply not aware of their deep-seated homosexual orientation at the time of marriage. This is especially true when they have little or no personal sexual experience. Others suspect that they might be gay or lesbian, and believe, or have been advised by others, that marriage is the solution to their problem. Some homosexual people marry on account of social pressures, family expectations, the desire to escape an intolerable home situation, disappointment with failed same-sex relationships, or even a strong desire for the permanency and stability that accompany married life. Gay and lesbian people also enter heterosexual partnerships out of a genuine affection or love for the other person and/or because of a strong desire for children and all the conventional acceptance and comforts of family life.

Others are very much aware of their homosexuality at the time of marriage and their conscious choice to marry heterosexually includes no illusion about the power of marriage to redirect their erotic preferences.

For some men, marriage does seem to work, at least for an extended period, as a way of coping with homosexuality. They hope the experience of a heterosexual relationship, a somewhat weak identification with the gay lifestyle, and minimal exposure to homosexual stimuli will be sufficient to cause their homosexual impulses eventually to disappear. Among these men are those who have had some previous homosexual relationships in their early years, but who now seem able to get beyond those attractions. However, after several years of marriage, possibly with the birth of children, they may find themselves struggling again with desires and fantasies they thought they had long ago left behind.

Many times personal, job-related, or family crises are enough to trigger homosexual feelings and behavior. At such times married gay men can find themselves under tremendous pressure to hide this part of their lives from others, including spouses. Typically, this is the case of the "pillar" of the parish, the community, the political or business world who engages in brief, furtive, sexual contacts accompanied by continual fear of discovery, arrest, or blackmail. The suburbanite who comes into the city occasionally, or even on a regular basis, for sexual contacts bordering on compulsive behavior, and the men who frequent the homosexual world on out-of-town trips are also good examples of this form of coping. Usually the tensions become so unbearable that, at some point, the individual seeks out temporary relief in the anonymity of the cathedral, confessional, or counseling center. The individual needs help to resolve the conflicts arising from a double life of deceit and guilt, and the poor self-image that such a lifestyle engenders.

Among women, however, there are significant differences in the coping strategies that seem to have less to do with sexual activity than with emotional relationships. Lesbian women who have married heterosexual men will speak of experiencing a deep and intense intimacy with another woman that is more fulfilling than they experienced with a husband. It often takes them a long time to arrive at the point where they describe these feelings and behavior in terms of homosexuality or lesbianism, and a greater time before they take on these terms as identities for themselves.

Just as validly, we can also ask why some heterosexual people knowingly marry homosexual individuals. There are cases, for example, in which a gay male tells an intended spouse that he thinks he might be homosexual and even indicates some reluctance to proceed with marriage plans. The intended spouse might respond that since she really loves him, she is willing to "take a chance." Some women might also believe that marriage will "change all that," or even that "sex isn't all that important anyway." These responses are unrealistic and ought to be exposed as such in order to prevent a great amount of trauma and pain later on. In what can only be considered an example of British understatement, the bishops of England and Wales in their 1979 guidelines for ministry to homosexual persons warn that "marriage has not proved to be a successful answer for most homosexuals" (Catholic Social Welfare Commission, 1981, p. 12).

Both the women's movement and the gay and lesbian liberation movement have had some impact on reducing the number of homosexual people who attempt heterosexual marriages. The latter movement, especially with the stress it places on personal authenticity and freedom in finding one's sexual identity, is helping some younger gay and lesbian people resist the pressures to marry heterosexually. Others though, while they strongly desire integrity, personal honesty, and self-identity as homosexual, are simply not strong enough to cope with their homosexuality except through marriage to an unsuspecting partner, especially when marriage is linked with advancement in the corporate structure of the business or political worlds. Such marriages will continue to occur and will require both psychological and spiritual ministries.

Ministering to Married Gay Men and Lesbian Women

Ministering to married homosexual people is one of the difficult pastoral challenges facing the church today. It is a challenge made especially traumatic and painful because other people, including spouses and children, are deeply affected by the tensions, conflicts, and painful decisions that must be made when homosexuality touches a marriage. Repeatedly married people speak of the helplessness they experience in trying to be honest with themselves while attempting to avoid hurting the people they live with and love.

The first difficulty in ministering to married people is determining whether the person affected is homosexual or is actually bisexual. The bisexual phenomenon has received relatively little attention from researchers, although many studies indicate that it is far more frequent than most people believe. The Kinsey studies, for example, indicated that 37% of the male population has some physical experience of homosexuality between adolescence and old age. If conscious sexual attraction is added to actual physical contact, the incidence is even greater. Kinsey (1948) concluded that "since only 50% of the population is exclusively heterosexual throughout its adult life, and since only 4% of the population is exclusively homosexual throughout its life, it appears that nearly half of the population (46%) engages in both heterosexual and homosexual activities or reacts to persons of both sexes in the course of their adult lives" (p. 656). The incidence of homosexuality among women was found to be one-third to one-half less than among men.

Bisexuality can be thought of as 1) real and natural; 2) transitory, i.e., the person will eventually return to his or her original orientation; 3) transitional, i.e., the person will become exclusive at the orientation opposite the original orientation; or 4) homosexual denial. If we consider that sexual orientation cannot be defined in terms of behavior, then the definition and analysis become even more complex. With regard to the moral issues surrounding bisexuality, only one author has attempted to spell out some of the responsibilities of the bisexual person in terms of freedom to develop and strengthen one's heterosexual component (Keane, 1977). Many times the help of a professional counselor will be required if the pastoral minister is not equipped to handle this area. Generally it is sound advice to tell an individual confused about his or her sexuality not to make any hasty decisions. He or she should continue with professional psychological help and pastoral counseling in order to arrive at the decision most appropriate for the person's own life as well as the lives of others who may be involved.

In cases of those determined to be exclusively or predominantly homosexual, there are other issues a pastoral counselor will have to help the individual resolve. If the spouse is unaware of the person's homosexuality, a decision must be made regarding whether that information should be shared and, if so, how best to proceed with the disclosure. There might be cases where the situation warrants not telling the spouse, at least immediately. If the spouse already knows, the counselor should provide support for that individual who faces the feelings of anger, confusion, and denial that inevitably accompany such a revelation. At times, the couple will approach the counselor together, but generally it is the homosexual person who first seeks help. In some major cities there are support groups for married gay and lesbian persons as well as groups for straight partners. It is well, though, for the counselor to be familiar with the philosophy and viewpoints of each group before recommending it to others.

Solutions to the Married Homosexual Dilemma

There are four possible solutions to the dilemma of married gay and lesbian persons. They are modification, platonic relationship, open relationship, and divorce/separation.

1. Modification An approach attempting to modify a particular situation claims to revert or convert homosexual orientation. Most of the time the "successes" relate only to a modification of behavior and not to the psychic responses, erotic attractions or fantasies. The Masters and Johnson claim of a 33% failure rate in changing homosexual people has been exposed as an incredible and unprofessional manipulation of statistics and as arbitrary definition of terms (Gramick and Nugent, 1979). The directors themselves refer to that part of the program as a disaster area (Masters and Johnson, 1979). False hopes that change is either possible or easily accomplished should not be held out to gay and lesbian people. In all fairness though, a counselor working with a bisexual person dissatisfied with his or her homosexual component could aid the individual in finding a reputable program or therapist to provide assistance in strengthening the heterosexual dimension. The motivations, age, life situation, and previous experiences are all important elements in the success or failure of such an attempt. We cannot uncritically dismiss valid and reputable attempts to help people alleviate tensions over homosexual behavior.

2. Platonic Relationship The platonic relationship strives to maintain and strengthen the marriage by love and affection expressed in sexual but nongenital ways. This is possible for some people as documented cases have proven. However, such a decision is unusual and can only be successfully implemented by a small number of people. The decision must be mutual, have support systems to sustain it, such as ongoing counseling and/or spiritual guidance, and should have a proven healthy influence on the total relationship. The ages of the people involved, their abilities to sublimate erotic energies, and their level of communication in other areas are crucial elements if such a solution is to work.

3. Open Relationship The open relationship allows for the gay or lesbian partner, and sometimes the heterosexual partner as well, to seek outside genital relationships with an understanding that these will not become an emotional threat to the primary commitment. Aside from the important ethical-moral dimensions of such a decision, these agreements, at least from the outside, seem to provide a workable solution. In most cases, however, the ultimate result is separation and divorce. In the Christian value system such a solution is judged morally unacceptable on the same grounds that the Christian tradition rejects adultery. Since the advent of the HIV-AIDS crisis, the open relationship is even more problematic and raises a host of questions about personal and social responsibility for one's sexual behavior.

4. Divorce/Separation At times, the Christian counselor reluctantly accepts divorce as being the only viable solution to an otherwise intolerable and harmful situation. It would be naive to expect any real or lasting success from attempts to support, and cruel to enforce, a marriage between a true gay or lesbian person and a heterosexual spouse. Canon lawyers still debate whether or not the Roman Catholic church should make constitutional and irreversible homosexuality an impediment to contracting valid sacramental marriage. In the meantime, tribunal practice allows for an annulment on the grounds of "psychic incapacity" or "psychological disorder" (Thomas, 1983). There is also one case on record in which the Vatican's Sacred Rota has granted an annulment on the grounds of bisexuality.

Making the decision to divorce or separate raises other issues for both partners. The church's pastoral outreach to separated and divorced persons can provide much support, especially for the non-homosexual spouse. Both usually struggle with questions such as how, or even whether, to tell friends and relatives the real reason for the breakup, or how to regain one's own self-confidence in the area of sexual identity, which may have been threatened or damaged by the experience of divorce. Along with the usual trauma of divorce, the non-homosexual partner has the added burden of self-questioning and doubt. "Did I hold on too tightly?" "Why wasn't I woman (or man) enough to hold the marriage together?" "Did I drive him (or her) away?" "Was I a cause of the homosexuality?" "Could I have prevented it?" A dramatic and unique reunion after a separation because of a husband's homosexuality is recounted in Carol Lynn Pearson's (1986) moving book, *Good-bye, I Love You*, the story of a wife who took her husband back and cared for him until his death from AIDS.

In cases where there are children, the couple must decide if the children are old enough to understand and, if so, how to tell them; and in telling them, how to ensure that the information is not used by one parent against the other to engender feelings of hatred or fear in the child. The anxiety that a non-gay parent experiences about how a developing child may be affected by the other parent's homosexuality cannot be dismissed easily. The pastoral minister should be ready to assist in responding to such issues as peer rejection, anger at the gay or lesbian parent, and the possible confusion and doubts the child may experience in regard to his or her own sexuality.

The issues of child custody and visitation rights are often grounds for long court battles and painful struggles between parents. I have discussed the legal picture in some detail toward the end of Chapter 1. The underlying issue is whether the homosexual orientation of one parent will directly affect the child's own sexuality. The relatively few studies done in this area indicate that a child's basic sexual orientation is not influenced by that of the parents. Related issues are gender identity, which is an inner sense of being male or female, and gender role, which was defined in Chapter 4. The central question, however, is the precise relationship between gender identity and sexual orientation development. Gender nonconformity seems to be a predictor of homosexual orientation. This issue is beginning to receive serious study (Bell, Weinberg and Hammersmith, 1981).

Preventive Approaches

The time to deal with homosexuality in marriage is before the marriage occurs. Two areas especially provide opportunities for ministry: marriage preparation and sex education programs. When a couple approaches a minister to discuss marriage plans which are to include discussions about sexuality, it is crucial that the couple be given an opportunity to deal with feelings and experiences of homosexuality. A sensitive counselor can raise the issue in non-threatening and helpful ways. Or an instrument such as the Pre-Marital Inventory developed by Bess Associates can be used, which asks each partner to respond to the item, "Homosexual tendencies in either one of us has me worried." Asking the couple how they might react to a lesbian or gay child is another way to tap their feelings about the topic.

No matter how it is done, an open discussion of the topic has many benefits. It can enhance and deepen the level of communication the couple is striving to build. It can help clear the air, especially for some males who carry minimal guilt feelings about adolescent same-sex behavior. Discussion can also help the couple deal comfortably with the homosexual component many people experience in their lives. Most importantly, discussion can help surface potential difficulties in the marriage, especially where the counselor detects hesitancy or strong denial when the topic arises. The counselor should always provide ample opportunity for either of the parties to have time alone to talk about homosexuality in a more in-depth manner if such seems necessary. In the case of individuals whom the counselor determines to be struggling with strong or persistent same-sex feelings or behavior, it is important to stress the inadvisability of marriage as long as such strong contraindications exist.

Finally, in the area of sex education, especially on junior and senior high levels, it is important that some part of the program be devoted to homosexuality and its impact on marriage and family life. Diocesan family life programs and offices, for instance, need to integrate a sensitive component on homosexuality in their educational outreaches and resources, especially those designed for parish use. Parents of gay or lesbian children and spouses married to gay or lesbian partners ought to be able to find sensitive treatment and competent resources within their own parishes. If these are unavailable, people should be referred to diocesan agencies and denominational resources that provide professional counseling or pastoral direction when it is required. A recommendation of the United States Catholic Conference (1981) calls for the diocese to make available at a parish level competent and trained counselors to minister to homosexually oriented Catholics including spouses.

Though many books on homosexuality contain a discussion of marriage, there is little available from the Roman Catholic perspective. As the issue begins to come to the fore in the consciousness of family ministers and church personnel, we can hope for the development of sound resources for couples coping with homosexuality in their unions as well as for those couples whose marriage has already ended. If we can learn to acknowledge and face the reality of the situation with sensitive understanding and sound pastoral principles, we can come to the aid of people who often suffer silently and alone and who feel caught in an impossible situation. We can also contribute substantially to the efforts of the church to strengthen and solidify the beautiful gift of God to humankind that is Christian marriage.

We can begin to implement the words of John Paul II (1981) who said in his Apostolic Exhortation on the Family, "The church's pastoral concern will not be limited only to the Christian families closest at hand; it will extend its horizons in harmony with the heart of Christ and will show itself to be even more lively for families in general and for those families in particular that are in difficult or irregular situations. For all of them the church will have a word of truth, goodness, understanding, hope and deep sympathy with their sometimes tragic difficulties" (p. 458).

PART THREE

RELIGIOUS AND CLERICAL LIFE

–7–

Surfacing the Issues

Although still a delicate and potentially explosive topic in the Catholic community, the issue of homosexuality, priesthood, and religious life is not a new one. Even before it was raised in the somewhat limited circles of national Catholic organizations in the 1970s, a priest pioneer in the field of counseling to gay clergy and religious carefully and cautiously tried to harmonize a sensitive approach to gay and lesbian persons with a consistent defense of the church's ban on homogenital behavior. Already in the 1960s and early 1970s, Rev. John Harvey, O.S.F.S., had published several articles on the vocation and counseling of gay religious.

In the late seventies a number of national Catholic religious organizations began in-house discussions of the topic of homosexuality and religious life. Since 1972, a group of about a dozen Christian Brothers had been meeting in a yearly seminar to study spirituality and gospel living in the post-Vatican II church. Their 1977 seminar on sexuality resulted in the booklet *Sexuality and Brotherhood*, containing a brilliant article by Gabriel Moran that peripherally addressed the subject of homosexuality and religious life. In his typically stimulating and provocative fashion, Moran (1977) wrote that religious life "might provide a stable setting for the working out of homosexual love" (p. 46). For Moran, religious organizations should be "a natural bridge for the meeting of straight and gay worlds" (p. 47).

In their seminar five years later, the same group of Christian Brothers published a booklet entitled *Prejudice*, which included theological and sociological considerations on homophobia. In his article on gay brothers, Martin Helldorfer (1982) identified the problem of silence surrounding the question of homosexuality and religious life. Helldorfer argued that this silence, born from fear, must be confronted in religious communities as a matter of justice.

Also in the late seventies the Jesuits began to explore the issue in their spirituality journal *Studies in the Spirituality of Jesuits* with a case study about the feelings of a newly ordained priest after a homogenital experience. The exploration included comments about sexual identity, counseling approaches, and appropriate spiritual direction. In 1978, the National Assembly of Religious Women published two brief interviews with lesbian nuns in their newsletter *Probe*. This was the first public acknowledgment of lesbianism among women religious.

Religious vocation and formation personnel also began to respond to the issue. In 1979, the National Conference of Religious Vocation Directors of Men published an article on gay candidates in their organizational journal *Call to Growth and Minis-*

try. Dignity began a preliminary dialogue with vocation and formation directors to ascertain their positions on the admission of openly gay and lesbian candidates. The Intercommunity Center for Justice and Peace in New York was likewise collecting data on the admission policies of religious congregations and diocesan seminaries in the New York metropolitan area.

While this incipient discussion and writing was being undertaken by religious organizations and congregations, two groups were founded in 1977 specifically to extend direct service and ministry to lesbian and gay priests and religious. One of these groups was Renewal, Rest and Re-creation begun by John Harvey to provide a retreat environment for priests and brothers who were troubled by their homosexuality. His view of homosexuality as a developmental disorder has met with great resistance from priests who accept the 1973 judgment of the American Psychiatric Association that homosexuality is a variant, not deviant form of sexuality. For example, when Francis Schulte, then Bishop of Wheeling, West Virginia, proposed that Harvey be invited to establish a ministry group in the diocese, an advisory board who listened to Harvey's approach rejected the idea.

In contrast, the basic philosophy of another group, Communication Ministry, assumes that lesbian and gay persons are not essentially disordered and can grow spiritually by mutual sharing and support. Communication Ministry began as a network mainly of gay priests and brothers who exchanged views on particular themes, such as celibacy and relationships, through the medium of a monthly newsletter. The organization has since offered annual retreats in various regions of the U.S. and has devoted three issues of its journal to AIDS, to seminary and religious formation, and to mid-life issues.

A third group founded in 1977, New Ways Ministry, also began to work with priests and religious as one part of its educational and pastoral ministry regarding homosexuality. In response to requests from women religious who had experienced a disproportionate number of males at retreats for homosexual religious, New Ways Ministry sponsored a retreat for lesbian nuns in 1979. In 1984-85, the organization conducted a series of regional workshops for women religious who were exploring their sexual orientation and in 1985-86 sponsored a series of symposiums for religious congregational leadership on the topic of homosexuality, priesthood, and religious life.

Religious organizations such as Maryknoll, the National Sisters Vocation Conference, the Religious Formation Conference, and the newly formed National Religious Vocation Conference addressed the topic in their respective journals or newsletters. Increasingly, the issue surfaced in the public forums of more mainline publications such as *The Priest, Review for Religious, Sisters Today,* and *Commonweal.* Portions of books or anthologies on homosexuality invariability contained chapters or contributions on religious life and priesthood. By 1983, a discussion document on sexuality from the Committee on Priestly Life and Ministry of the National Conference of Catholic Bishops even contained a case study about a gay priest.

Initially, most of the literature discussing gay religious and clergy, as well as pastoral ministry to these individuals, was directed to priests and brothers. Women religious were usually an afterthought. But by 1985 lesbian nuns had gained widespread interest and attention not only in Catholic circles, but in the world at large because of extensive publicity surrounding the publication of the book *Lesbian Nuns: Breaking Silence* (Curb and Manahan, 1985). The title was somewhat misleading because most of the essays were contributed by former nuns. Although this collective work received less than enthusiastic reviews from the *National Catholic Reporter* and *Sisters Today,* its real value lay in drawing public attention to this neglected women's issue. Another book, *Immodest Acts*, a carefully researched historical account of a seventh century lesbian nun, appealed to scholars and students of history (Brown, 1986). An article that appeared in *Women and Therapy* in 1986, titled "Counseling Lesbian Women Religious," was helpful to the religious professional (Murphy, 1986). However, neither the historical work nor the counseling article had as significant an effect on the general public as the much ballyhooed trade book *Lesbian Nuns: Breaking Silence*.

Public awareness of gay priests has been aroused recently by a plethora of print media accounts and TV talk shows on the problem of clerical pedophilia. Although adult homosexuality and pedophilia are distinct clinical categories, gay priests have unfortunately been linked to this dysfunctional behavior in the public's mind. However, some sensitive articles dealing with gay clergy have appeared in Catholic newspapers beginning with a 1976 interview with an anonymous gay priest in the *National Catholic Reporter*. Since then this newspaper has periodically published opinion pieces and news items on gay priests and brothers in a generally balanced manner. Several years ago two books on the topic were published that further contributed to opening the doors of silence that have blocked a healthy discussion of sexuality and homosexuality in some church circles (Gramick, 1989; Wolf, 1989).

The events, organizations, and resources described above began to surface publicly the issue of lesbian and gay clergy and religious. What are some of the specific concerns that church administrators, as well as gay and lesbian religious and clergy, sought to address? It seems that certain questions continually arise. For example, how does a sister, brother, or priest know if he or she is gay or lesbian? How many gay priests and brothers and lesbian nuns are there?

For young men entering religious life today or for those men already in religious life, knowing and naming their sexual orientation have most probably already occurred since males generally become aware of their sexual orientation at puberty or in their early teens. For reasons probably related to biological maturation, boys develop sexual curiosity and interests at a younger age than girls do.

Females generally discover their sexual identity around the age of 21. Since most nuns entered religious life as teenagers, most would have assumed that they were heterosexual and probably proceeded into a formation program that stunted their sexual growth. Today's young women seeking entrance into religious life are generally older than 21 and may already have discovered their lesbian orientation. However, the problem of sexual identification remains a concern even among young women in formation. The frequent question heard among women religious is, "How do I know if I'm lesbian?"

What Homosexuality Is Not

Before exploring the dynamics of homosexual orientation, it would be helpful to consider what is not a homosexual orientation, but what is often confused as homosexuality. Living and working in a homosocial environment does not necessarily mean that a person is lesbian or gay. Expressing human affection by touching, hugging, and dispassionate kissing with someone of the same gender does not indicate homosexuality nor is it a display of immaturity. One of the hazards of a traditional celibate lifestyle is the risk of losing natural warmth and affection through the fear of touching or holding others.

Homosexuality should not be confused with exclusive relationships that should be recognized for what they are: relationships that separate two people in an unhealthy way from the rest of the community, one person often being extremely emotionally dependent on the other. Exclusive relationships can occur between two persons of any orientation. A friendship that allows room only for each other is hurtful, not only to community life but also to the persons involved. Most religious have seen these neurotic dyads in communities. While describing the divisiveness caused by exclusivity in community life may be theoretically easy, caution must be exercised in order to avoid labeling a healthy friendship as divisive or exclusive. Friends need time alone together for the relationship to grow. Feelings of jealousy can subconsciously motivate individuals to criticize or resent a wholesome relationship between two people, especially if the individual desires a closer friendship with one or the other person.

Living with only one other person of one's own gender, even for many years, does not automatically mean that a person is lesbian or gay. Because of new ministries in far flung geographic areas where communities were not previously established, because of a shift away from large institutional living in favor of smaller, close-knit groups, and because of a desire to develop more meaningful and less formal relationships, many religious, especially women, are living as Jesus commissioned his disciples in the Gospel: "two by two." Given the social fabric and congregational ministerial goals, the numbers of such living and/or working teams will probably increase as we approach the second millennium. While some of these couple relationships may be genuine gay or lesbian relationships, it would be a grave mistake to assume that all or even most automatically are. Such couple relationships must be accorded the respect of friendship by community members, while the coupled religious should be enthusiastic about including other community members in their day-to-day lives.

Homosexuality should not be equated with same-sex friendships, which will always exist in religious life. Instead of formally condemning "particular friendships" as in the past, community members are learning a healthy respect for same-gender friendships. A blessing to religious communities, these friendships energize and empower their members to dedicate their time and talents to serving God's people. They counteract the almost 100% professional atmosphere in which most religious live. Intimate relationships enable individuals to discover who they really are and where their values lie. By providing opportunities to exercise receptivity as well as independence, close human relationships awaken a person's capacity to care and to love.

Same-gender friendships are not common among American males probably because it is difficult for the American male to distinguish and separate same-gender friendship from a gay relationship. But many women enjoy close friendships with other women. In American culture and in most of the world's societies, intimate friendships among women are socially acceptable. Heterosexual women do not usually entertain questions of deep eroticism when they reflect on their female-female relationships. They have strong emotional ties to their female friends, but if they experience any romantic attractions, these kinds of feelings do not long endure.

So we see that homosexual relationships are not the same as exclusive relationships, living or working couple relationships, or same-gender friendships although lesbian and gay religious could find themselves in any of these situations. Lesbian and gay religious experience the same needs for love, touch, and affection that heterosexuals do. They treasure deep friendships with heterosexuals with whom they are not romantically involved. They struggle, as heterosexuals do, to free their relationships from suffocating domination, control, and exclusivity. And some have lived with another lesbian or gay religious with whom they develop a close friendship and deep bond.

Being Lesbian or Gay

Who, then, is a lesbian or gay person? Until the second half of the twentieth century, sexual researchers defined a lesbian or gay individual in behavioral terms, i.e., an individual's orientation depended on genital contact or on "having sex" with another person of the same gender. Therefore, someone who engaged in same-sex genital activity, no matter how often or how infrequently, was labelled homosexual. Since bisexuals and heterosexuals were similarly defined according to genital behavior, virgins lacked a sexual orientation by such a definition.

The misconception that being lesbian or gay requires homogenital behavior was made evident during a 1979 retreat for lesbian nuns sponsored by New Ways Ministry. Questions by a number of church representatives indicated that these church officials assumed that the nuns were sexually active. Cardinal William Baum of Washington, D.C., complained about the retreat to the Sacred Congregation for Religious and Secular Institutes at the Vatican. This curial office subsequently issued a set of unsigned "Observations" about the retreat, which was sent with a cover letter from the Secretary of the Congregation to our religious superiors. Most of the document decried the "goals of the homosexual culture," which were equated with the "acceptance of and justification of homosexual activity." The Observations claimed that individual participants would experience "potential spiritual harm" from "confused guidance" because the "retreat facilitator will be a gay sister." It stated that "scandal" was "likely to be given by the example of religious women forming a homosexual group with its at least implicit public support for the goals of the homosexual culture." Coming out as "gay and celibate" was judged to be a "slogan" used by religious unless they made a "clear reaffirmation of church teaching on the morality of homosexuality." The entire document betrayed a preoccupation with homogenital activity.

Because many people mistakenly equate lesbian and gay identity with homogenital activity, there are probably many religious who would refuse to name themselves lesbian or gay because they are sexually abstinent. Consider a parallel situation. If religious do not engage in opposite-sex genital activity, how can they know they are heterosexual? In each case, the answer lies in being aware of one's physical, erotic, and romantic feelings, fantasies, and desires.

Kinsey believed that there was a continuum of sexual orientation from exclusively heterosexual at one pole to exclusively homosexual at the other. What determines one's position on this orientation rating scale? Certainly not genital behavior, as was once believed. This is evident because approximately one fourth of gay males have experienced heterosexual intercourse and about one third of lesbian women are biological mothers. If genital activity does not determine sexual orientation, what does?

A person's sexual orientation depends on one's primary erotic, emotional, psychological, and social interest, even though that interest may not be overtly expressed. Traditionally, the primary emotional, psychological, and social interest of most religious has been other community members. But these elements *alone* are insufficient to define a person as a lesbian or gay individual. An *erotic* interest must also be present. Most religious have suppressed or repressed their homosexual as well as heterosexual erotic instincts. There is little open discussion of romantic or sexual feeling, fantasies, and desires in many religious communities of men and in most religious communities of women. In the absence of an erotic dimension it is impossible to categorize a person's sexual orientation. Kinsey found that 14% of the female population and 1% of the male population had no sexual orientation whatsoever. They reported that they had no erotic or romantic interests or activity. Given the sexual revolution in the decades subsequent to Kinsey's collection of data, the proportion of asexual persons in the general population today may be somewhat lower, although Kinsey's percentages may be valid for those already in religious life.

Rev. Paul Shanley, the Boston "street priest" of the 1960s, used to point out that almost everyone has a sexual "major" and a "minor." Many, if not most, basically heterosexual persons experience some degree of same-sex feelings, fantasies, desires, or attractions. If heterosexual persons interact in an exclusively or primarily homosocial environment for a long period of time, it is only natural that their same-sex instincts, even minimal ones, will become evident. This explains, in part, the increased incidence of homosexual behavior among military personnel, prisoners, or other persons enclosed in a same-sex environment. Most return to heterosexual behavior when they are removed from their homosocial setting.

Unless an individual is aware of his or her orientation prior to entrance into a primarily homosocial atmosphere, discovering one's sexual identity may be difficult and confusing. This is especially the case for women religious. Experiencing sexual and romantic feelings toward other community members is quite natural and normal. However, if these feelings are extremely intense, perdure over long periods of time, and occur frequently with different persons in the course of a person's religious life, one's sexual identity is most likely primarily lesbian or gay.

What constitutes homosexuality, then, is a deep, intense, erotic instinct or feeling for persons of the same gender, which translates into strong sexual desire and possibly actions when the "right person" comes along. Lesbian and gay people fall in love just as heterosexual people do; the only difference is that they fall in love with someone of their own gender. Being lesbian or gay does not mean sexual attraction to *every* person of one's own gender. Falling in love with numerous persons of one's own gender over the years is a good indication of homosexuality. Having sexual affairs is unnecessary; examining sexual feelings, fantasies, and romantic desires will bring this kind of awareness.

Incidence

An erroneous notion, quite common even among many Catholics, is that all, or practically all, religious are homosexual. In a lecture about homosexuality and the clergy delivered at a 1985 New Ways Ministry symposium in Washington, D.C., John Boswell remarked that most non-Christian observers of Roman Catholicism in the Middle Ages believed that the celibate clergy was overwhelmingly gay. During the Middle Ages many believed that the debate about mandatory celibacy was influenced by a political struggle between a heterosexual married clergy and a gay clergy who were in ecclesiastical control. As Boswell indicates, the truth of these assertions cannot be proven historically. But the belief that clergy and religious are overwhelming gay and lesbian persists today.

A 1985 survey by the National Conference of Religious Vocation Directors (1986) revealed that 1% of the women and 5% of the men admitted during 1980-85 into postulancy or residency programs acknowledged to their formation leaders a lesbian or gay orientation. These figures pertain only to those in the early stages of religious formation or clerical vocation discernment and rely on information actually shared with authority figures. It is quite possible, even probable, that the actual numbers and percentages of lesbian and gay religious or clergy are much higher. There is no comparable survey of diocesan seminaries at the present time.

In the absence of any reliable data on the incidence of lesbian or gay persons in religious life today, we have only estimates from church workers and ecclesial administrators who deal with lesbian or gay members. For example, A.W. Richard Sipe (1990), a resigned priest and therapist, estimates that approximately 20% of priests or brothers are gay. Others have advanced estimates of 30% or even 50%. Unlike the general population where gay men may outnumber lesbian women two to one, in religious life and priesthood the numbers of gay priests and brothers probably exceeds the number of lesbian nuns by far more than two to one according to church personnel in the field. If the mailing list of Communication Ministry serves as a random sample, the ratio of gay male religious to lesbian nuns is more than ten to one. This may mean that the percentage of priests and brothers is much higher than the 10-16% estimated in the general male population and/or that the percentage of lesbian nuns is lower than the 7-8% estimated in the general female population.

At present it is difficult to advance even a tentative suggestion concerning the number of lesbian nuns. Any estimate may be premature and misleading because women religious are just beginning to address personal, sexual issues in their congregations. Although nuns have publicly identified with the rights of sexual minorities and with raising controversial sexual issues such as women's ordination, abortion, and tubal ligation, the discussion for them has been mostly objective and academic.

Many nuns are in Kinsey's category "x," i.e., asexual. There are logical reasons to explain this assertion. The fact that the median age in most congregations of women religious was 65 in 1989 implies that most nuns entered community life prior to the period of renewal following the Second Vatican Council (Tri-Conference Retirement Office, 1990). It was an era in which young girls commonly entered the convent between the ages of 14 and 18, generally prior to the time when lesbian women come to an awareness of their sexual orientation. It was an era in which most formation programs did not include a consideration of personal, sexual issues. It was an era in which candidates and postulants were warned to avoid sexual feelings as an occasion of sin. It was an era in which there was no in-depth understanding of sexuality in society at large.

Only since the 1980s have some religious congregations of women begun to address sexual issues in ways that reflect their own experiences of sexuality. It is generally religious who are younger than 65 who take advantage of programs, workshops, or institutes about sexuality that some congregations have sponsored. It may be an impossible goal to expect that the majority of women religious will eventually examine their own sexual feelings, needs, and desires to come to an understanding of their sexual orientation. As women religious increasingly analyze their own sexual stories, more sisters will probably claim a lesbian identity.

I believe the time has come to surface more publicly and in greater depth the issues surrounding homosexuality, priesthood, and religious life. It is a time in which many in the church suspect that the great resistance to and suppression of any development regarding sexual issues within some segments of the hierarchy are due to an unwillingness to face homosexuality within its own ranks. It is a time in which lesbian nuns and gay priests and brothers are claiming their own pride and goodness and following the Gospel mandate to let their lights shine instead of hiding them under a bushel or in a closet (Matt. 5:14-16). It is a time in which the faith community may be ready and willing to listen to and actually hear the voices of the lesbian and gay ministers in our midst. It is time to acknowledge that lesbian and gay religious and clergy are an important and vital part of the Body of Christ.

–8–

Seminary and
Religious Candidates

In the film version of the Broadway play *Mass Appeal* there is a tense and explosive confrontation between a seminary rector and the pastor of a local parish. Charles Durning, the actor who plays the rector, challenges the pastor's (Jack Lemmon's) defense of a student working as an intern at the pastor's posh suburban rectory. The young deacon has already run afoul of the rector for defending two other seminarians suspected of a homosexual relationship. The deacon's own sexuality has been a topic of a conversation between the deacon and the rector, who has his own suspicions. "We have too many priests out of the closet already and too many others still in," Durning yells at Lemmon. "And this one was out and now he's back in."

Growing Concern About Gay Applicants

In this case, film art imitates the reality of contemporary Catholic life, where there is a growing concern about homosexual candidates for priesthood and religious life. The two primary reasons for this concern are the increasing numbers of self-identified and self-affirming gay male applicants and the growing visibility and outspokenness of gay clergy in the secular and Catholic media. Related but distinct issues are the publicity surrounding some arrests of Catholic clerics by police for illegal sexual activity, numerous civil lawsuits against dioceses and orders for sexual misconduct by some priests and brothers, and the appearance of HIV-AIDS.

There have been several widely publicized AIDS cases involving the deaths of priests. In Seattle, homosexual activity as the actual cause of AIDS was acknowledged publicly by one priest's superior to the parish community. In 1988 the Conference of Major Superiors of Men and the Catholic Health Association jointly produced a videotape for selected audiences about AIDS within the U.S. Catholic priesthood and brotherhood. The on-camera interviews with religious diagnosed with AIDS and with their congregational leaders were candid and sensitive. Fortunately, most religious groups have responded with courage and compassion to members with AIDS despite some sensational publicity. In some cities special treatment and care centers for priests and religious with AIDS have been established.

Some dioceses and religious orders have begun mandatory HIV-testing of all applicants. Others have opposed such testing because of serious questions about the reliability of tests, potential breaches of confidentiality, and a witch-hunt mentality that could use the testing to eliminate _a priori_ all gay candidates. The argument that dioceses and orders need to have complete information on the health and physical condition of the candidate to determine the potential for ministry seems reasonable. The institution's financial responsibility for health care for the person is another consideration. But it would be disappointing to think that the decision to admit or reject an applicant was made solely on economic grounds. There are already precedents of the church's accepting other individuals with health problems such as multiple sclerosis. The photograph of a seminarian being ordained in a wheelchair is no longer the novelty it once was.

Broad-based testing has ethical implications for the individual and the community and ought not to be undertaken lightly or without serious discussion. The progress of those who test positive is increasing with new medical advances; there are reported cases of individuals living with AIDS for more than five years. The community or diocese must ask itself what help will be provided for those who test positive whether they are rejected or accepted. If testing is being considered, justice would require that: 1) if mandatory testing is inaugurated, _all_ candidates be tested; 2) the testing be as accurate as possible with allowances for false results; 3) distinctions be made between those who test positive for the antibody, and those who test positive for the AIDS virus itself; 4) the results be kept in as strict confidence as possible; 5) admission decisions not be made solely on the results of testing; 6) the person who tests positive not be required to reveal the manner of being exposed to the virus; 7) the institution give serious thought to accepting candidates with AIDS to witness to the mysterious workings of God's grace in a vulnerable humanity.

A new model of ministry to persons with AIDS (PWAs) is a religious community composed of people who themselves test HIV positive or who have AIDS. Damien Ministries in Washington,

D.C., is one such religious community. Is it possible that one day such a religious family will be recognized by church authorities? Would that be the voice of God speaking through this crisis? Would such a religious order be any more singular than the ragged band of Francis living with the poor, roaming the country-side, begging food, and shattering all the traditional concepts of religious life then known?

Apart from the growing concern over HIV-AIDS, the application of gay candidates raises a number of issues for the seminary or religious congregation and many others regarding the individual applicant. I would like to consider five issues in each area.

Issues for the Seminary and Religious Congregation

The first issue to be addressed is the question of homophobia. The fear of homosexuality can be based on ignorance, myths, stereotypes, past traumatic experiences, unconfronted sexual issues in one's life, and numerous other sources. Homophobia is not limited to heterosexual people. Self-hatred, a poor self-image, and neurotic guilt may be traced to homophobia in homosexual individuals themselves. Homophobia may range from a general feeling of uncomfortability about the topic to an emotional hostility that can erupt in violence. Active participation in ridicule or derogatory remarks about gay and lesbian people, studied ignorance about homosexuality, and even avoidance of the topic are all indications of some forms of homophobia.

Homophobia is the reverse side of homosexuality because the same questions and issues arise: what causes homophobia, what are its common manifestations, can the homophobic individual be changed, what are the personality characteristics of the homophobic individual? However, homophobia itself often prevents people from a calm, rational, and objective approach to the topic. It also prevents individuals from personal relationships with lesbian and gay people. Thus, the vicious circle continues: _ignorance breeds fear and isolation; isolation breeds more ignorance and fear._

The second issue is the need for the group to examine and clarify official and unofficial policies regarding gay applicants. Several groups have already undertaken such a process with benefit to all concerned. It is crucial to examine the existence and impact of homophobia in formulating policies that are realistic, just, and pastoral. Although many groups have avoided the issue of written policies, there is some indication that the Vatican agencies concerned with formation prefer that policies on homosexuality be articulated. One danger to be avoided is a written policy that does not embody the best experiences of communities and the best of scientific and sociological data.

A written policy has several advantages. It requires that a group confront issues as honestly as possible with the aid of contemporary scientific, theological, and pastoral data. It validates the issue, gives people permission to talk comfortably about homosexuality, and makes homophobia education easier to implement. With a written policy a potential member has some idea of what to expect in terms of support, institutional living, celibacy, and continued growth and development in this particular environment.

An objection we often hear is that there is no need for "special policies" for any group, and that they could even be a form of discrimination. Yet there are policies for newer kinds of applicants, such as previously married applicants, applicants with histories of alcohol or chemical abuse, and older applicants. Given the problems and stresses that lesbian women and gay men face in our homonegative societies and churches, it would be unrealistic and naive to think that they arrive at our doors with basically the same experiences of affirmation that heterosexual applicants bring.

A third challenge is to guarantee equality in the screening process of both homosexual and heterosexual candidates, while realizing that there might be particular areas unique to the gay applicant. The problem with some screening processes is that the voluntary sharing of one's homosexual identity with authorities is often sufficient reason to consider a person a poor risk or in need of being examined carefully. Ironically, the poor risk, who might be a rather integrated, self-affirming individual, is monitored closely while the not-so-evident, closeted or repressed homosexual applicant with far more serious affective and intellectual problems is allowed to advance unchallenged.

A screening process involves more than personal interviews, psychological tests, and even the standard contact programs or living experiences. It begins with the initial contact, continues through the formation period and years of study up to ordination and/or final vows. The process should not violate personal privacy or pry into every thought, word and deed of the candidate. An effective process provides an atmosphere of openness and trust about human sexuality, intimacy, and relationships which empowers individuals to discern freely the actions of God's grace as it mixes with their unique personalities and sexual journeys. This kind of ongoing process is both demanding and arduous, but there is no simple replacement to insure that candidates are given the professional, spiritual, and pastoral helps that will most effectively bring high caliber ministers into the service of the church.

Some gay candidates are challenging us to explore appropriate expressions of sexuality and intimacy in religious life. This may be the case because male sexuality has been socialized predominately in terms of genitality, competitiveness, and patriarchal models of relationships. A good screening process will encourage a healthy development of sexuality and intimacy while recognizing counterfeits or rationalizations for narcissistic behavior.

The fourth issue has to do with the integration of the gay candidate into the larger group. John Boswell has argued that clerical and religious life has traditionally been a benign place where homosexual people were free to explore and develop the dynamic relationship between their sexuality and faith lives. The contemporary concern by writers such as Andrew Greeley and Richard McBrien about the disproportionately large number of gay men in priesthood and religious life implies some kind of danger to the church. Rarely are the more positive reasons for such a phenomenon examined.

One basic fear often expressed in a somewhat sexist figure of speech is a homosexual version of the "rooster in the hen house" scenario. "Isn't it unfair or dangerous to put the homosexual person in a same-sex environment? Wouldn't this mean temptations against chastity for the gay candidate? Wouldn't it be a source of stress for all concerned?" The two false underlying assumptions in this concern are that gay people are sexually attracted to all other gay persons and that gay candidates are less easily able to direct and control their sexual urges. There is a false belief that homosexual individuals do not discriminate in their choice of partners while heterosexuals do.

Tension may arise when a gay individual, who is comfortable in his sexuality and perhaps somewhat open about it, is assigned to a particular living situation or ministry. Homophobia, seduction by another member who has not dealt with sexuality in a healthy manner, or other kinds of passive-aggressive forms of relating may ensue. On the other hand, the rectory or community in which the homosexual members are seen as dominating and forming closed subgroups can generate friction, a sense of isolation, and even powerlessness on the part of heterosexual members. A healthy resolution of these tensions depends a great deal on the maturity level of the gay members, the absence of homophobia in other members, the comfort level of leaders to face these issues openly, and the application of some basic principles and techniques of conflict resolution.

Integrating gay applicants into seminary or community life involves many of the same issues as integrating racial and ethnic minorities. Unfortunately, our track record here leaves much to be desired. Racism and homophobia are not entirely unrelated. One obvious difference is that we cannot ignore the presence of people of different racial and ethnic backgrounds because of their visibility, which can often prevent us from expressing the remnants of racism. Gay people, however, can suffer silently from the destructive and ugly sentiments, remarks, and policies of homophobic persons if they are especially anxious not to be known as homosexual.

A significant element of the process of integration is the continued education of diocesan personnel and community members despite the fact that people cannot be totally reasoned out of a position grounded on emotion. The best weapon against homophobia is knowing personally and relating with an integrated and healthy gay person. If the subject can be raised and discussed responsibly in newsletters, study days, and pastoral letters, then the task of integrating and affirming gay candidates and members is furthered.

The fifth issue is examining honestly what demands will be made on our seminaries and communities by the acceptance of homosexual candidates, especially those who are open about their sexuality. Some members fear that a diocese or congregation with a liberal admissions policy will quickly acquire an image or reputation for being a gay seminary or community. It can be especially painful and threatening to heterosexual members even when it is said in jest.

One response to this objection is to examine the underlying

fears. What does it really matter even if most of the priests or members are gay? The answer, of course, depends on what psychological, social, and theological judgments are made about homosexuality. If a homosexual orientation is "a developmental abnormality" as some claim (Harvey, 1987, p. 38), then there are reasons for concern. If, however, it is a variation of normal human sexual development for a certain number of people, well within the range of healthy sexuality, then other stances are possible. The resolution of these questions goes to the heart of contemporary controversies about homosexuality. There seems to be no common agreement about how to resolve these questions. In the meantime, however, people's fears about homosexuality need to be addressed no matter how fundamental or misplaced they might be.

There have been instances of immature and irresponsible homosexual behavior in seminary and religious life. But the basic point here is to recognize that the problem is not sexual orientation but irresponsible expressions. These irresponsible behaviors are often traced to emotional problems, poor self-image, addiction and/or psychological conflicts.

A seminary or religious congregation is committed to support a hurting member with institutional resources. In the struggle for sexual integration and a healthy celibacy some mistakes are to be expected. Some may become known to the general public. Yet true compassion and loyalty demand that the membership and authorities stand with the individual who might be angry, confused, hurt, and even incarcerated. Past experiences of disruptions or tensions, such as arrests or some other kind of exposure that have a negative effect on group morale can make a diocese or congregation wary of accepting gay candidates. It would be both unfortunate and unjust if such experiences and projected fears were allowed to dictate admission policies. The way a group responds to such situations is a real test of its willingness to undergo a potential spiritual growth that can rightfully be described as a passion experience.

Issues of Applicants

The first issue to be raised regarding the homosexually oriented applicant is the question of motivation. Those responsible for evaluation need a clear idea of why this individual is coming to a particular group and what are his underlying expectations of diocesan or community life, public ministry, and spirituality.

There is some evidence that many homosexual males tend to be drawn to priesthood or religious life out of a desire for pre-Vatican II models of structures, customs, and worship. Some candidates are seeking more traditional lifestyles and ministry with clearly defined roles, titles, areas of responsibility and clergy/lay distinctions. Some homosexual male applicants are not motivated by a need for same-gender environment as much as by a need for personal identity, structural security, and ecclesiastical approval. They are less interested in social justice ministry than sacramental ministry, more drawn to personal witness than social leadership, and less eager to promote collaboration with lay leadership. Although they often partake of the benefits of the gay culture, they are hostile critics of dissenting moral theologians, other religious who are more open about their sexuality, or those involved with ministry to lesbian and gay people. When these individuals reach positions of power and influence, they can inflict serious damage. Internalized homophobia is not necessarily related to a conservative or more traditional mind set, but the presence of the latter demands a serious look at the former.

However, motivations can and do change over time. Exposure to a diocese or congregation that is struggling to renew itself and to equip itself with new tools for a different period of history will have an important effect on its members. Earlier and less mature motivations can be transformed into more secure and gospel-based reasons for remaining with a particular group.

A second issue regarding the gay applicant involves an assessment of the individual's mechanisms for coping with a homosexual orientation. An individual can deal with his homosexuality by self-acceptance and affirmation or by denial, repression, and guilt. Does the person have a good self-image? How has he handled residual anger at the church or others? How necessary is it for the person to share his homosexual identity with others? Could any past behavior or relationships indicate a less than healthy integration of sexuality?

More problematic is the applicant who attempts to deny or repress a homosexual component, previous experiences, or relationships. While some might be denied admittance on these grounds, others might find in the seminary or community a safe place to work on these areas. Few candidates come with a completely integrated sexuality. It would be a worthy ministry for groups to be willing to spend time and resources in helping such people grow emotionally and spiritually, even though at a certain point in their integration the applicants may opt for other lifestyles.

Thirdly, the question of celibacy is important for the gay candidate to consider. The applicant needs some common understanding of the intellectual and affective meanings and parameters of celibacy as understood by this diocese or congregation. We have to face the new reality that some people come to the seminary or religious life either with an entirely different working definition of celibacy or with simply an *a priori* rejection of the traditional understanding which excludes genital intimacy. A diocese or congregation that adheres to the traditional understanding of celibacy needs to find ways to present that understanding clearly to the candidates during the admission process. This should be done as convincingly and as sensitively as possible without making either too much or too little of the question of genitality as one component of traditional celibacy.

The issue of previous genital relationships has been discussed in some of the literature on vocations, but not all can agree in establishing a certain trial time period for the candidate to prove his ability to live a celibate life. Some have suggested two or three years; most would agree that a person fresh from a sustained pattern of genital sexuality would not make a promising candidate for a celibate commitment. But such a principle would have excluded Thomas Merton from the Cistercians and did indeed exclude him from the Franciscans. "Celibacy takes a little getting used to," he once remarked.

The seminary or community should provide solid theological, ascetical, and spiritual formation to support an integrated celibate lifestyle. Formation in healthy celibacy has been woefully inadequate in the past. All too often those who have achieved the ideal are reluctant to serve as role models. We are only beginning to map out the terrain of healthy celibacy (Sipe, 1991). At any point along the journey the person can come to the conclusion that his understanding is incompatible with that of the group. In any case, an atmosphere of trust and openness has to be established from the very beginning.

Current feminist approaches to celibacy place primary emphasis not on the presence or absence of genitality, but on the right ordering of relationships. Drawing the line at genital sex, for them, is a typical patriarchal preoccupation with genitals and a truncated understanding of human sexuality. This approach, as well as the more traditional or mainstream one, will continue to be developed by writers as they explore the historical, theological, and experiential aspects of celibacy.

The need for support systems is a fourth issue that should be raised regarding the gay candidate. In a particularly homophobic or isolating setting, a homosexual person needs an atmosphere where feelings of self-affirmation, self-worth, and comfortability are promoted. What degree of involvement, for example, has the candidate had with gay social, religious, and political groups?

If an individual has established a strong network of gay and lesbian friends over the years, he will certainly expect to maintain contact with some of them and expect that they will be welcomed into the seminary or congregation's houses with warmth and hospitality. For some, the institutions of the local gay and lesbian community will provide support and fellowship; for others, an affiliation with groups like Communication Ministry or the Christian Community Association will suffice. For women religious the Conference for Catholic Lesbians and the Womanjourney retreats provide similar support.

There are, however, definite expectations and requirements of formation communities, such as presence, participation, and priorities. If a candidate has a strong need for identifying with the gay community and for support systems outside a seminary or congregation, the quality of community life and later ministry could suffer as a result. This happens in groups where there is little internal support, a grudging toleration, or even overt hostility. In these cases people will either leave or seek affirmation outside the group. Even internal support can take the forms of possessive dyads, cliques, and other tensions that can endanger the spirit of the community. To obviate these problems a seminary or congregation can initiate a support group for its homosexual members which can provide days of prayer and reflection, discussion opportunities, peer counseling, and socializing. Several congregations of men religious have already instituted such groups, although not always without some initial hesitation and tension.

Such a group benefits the well being of the whole congregation by combatting homophobia. What particular forms these groups take can vary widely depending on locations, resources, and other factors. The common element in all of them is a feeling of validation, respect, and support from within one's own religious family.

Concerns raised by these support groups are fears of a separatist group, dangers of "temptations to overt behavior" and "what if the bishop finds out?" In speaking to one congregation with a sizeable African American membership, I drew on an analogy between their prior support for a Black caucus in the congregation and their present fears about a gay support group. They saw the strong parallels immediately and admitted that part of the struggle was the fact that sexuality was involved with one kind of group and not the other.

There are a number of diocesan and religious support groups for homosexual men, but relatively few groups for women. The experiences of male homosexuality and lesbianism differ substantially. What does not differ, however, is the sense of group acceptance, personal affirmation and inner healing with the self, the church, and one's religious family. The potential impact for good on one's psychological and spiritual health and a renewed sense of ministry and commitment cannot be underestimated.

Finally, the issue of what kind of ministry the gay applicant feels called to can be broached even in the beginning stages of formation. It is impossible, of course, to determine precisely in what ministry this individual might be engaged in coming years. What is important is that the candidate is seeking the kind of ministry that the diocese or congregation is promoting. It would be a mistake for someone to seek admission solely because this group is "open to taking homosexual candidates." A congregation, for example, that is known for fairness in dealing with gay candidates may attract individuals who, because of their traits and talents, might actually be better suited to another group whose ministries are more in line with the applicant's interests.

Missionary groups with houses or ministries abroad must decide whether to accept a gay candidate if the only placement would be one that would cause undue stress on both the person and the local community. A homosexual priest in a one-priest parish, for example, in a predominantly fundamental and Protestant area would pose problems of personal support and public scrutiny for the person. What might be acceptable in a more urban location could prove problematic in another part of the country. Although this practical issue needs to be considered, it should not be employed simply as a reason for excluding gay candidates.

Other issues relating to forms of public ministry include whether the person feels called to work with the gay and lesbian population, whether he needs a certain amount of public visibility as a homosexual individual, what impact this has on the diocese or religious community, and the individual's stance on the church's teaching on homosexuality. If the candidate feels church teaching is inadequate, how will he give public witness to this teaching as a minister representing the church? Gerald Coleman (1984) believes that it is a matter of moral justice that the candidate "is willing and able to publicly profess the church's official teaching on the morality of homosexual behavior" and that a true incapacity here would be a "countersign for acceptance as a candidate" (p. 18). I would be willing to concede this requirement only if we would apply the same test to other moral areas like contraception, tubal ligation, and *in vitro* fertilization.

Conclusion

It would be less than honest to conclude this discussion on seminary and religious candidates without acknowledging that all of the above issues have been aggravated by the 1986 Vatican letter on homosexuality that called the homosexual condition an objective disorder (Nugent, 1988). If a gay candidate has accepted this teaching, how has this affected his own sense of self-worth? It remains extremely difficult to build a positive sense of self-acceptance in an area as crucial as one's human sexuality in light of such a negative judgment about homosexual identity. The self-affirming gay candidate to religious life today faces considerable hurdles to live honestly, openly, and integrally in the present climate of the church. Those seminaries and congregations that accept gay candidates and actively promote their growth must be prepared to face political and personal forces that militate against the fostering of mature, celibate, homosexual religious. But for those working with gay or lesbian people in religious life, there is a growing body of more positive Catholic teaching, which will be discussed in Chapter 10.

–9–

Lesbian Nuns and Midlife Transition

In their theories of personality development, Sigmund Freud, and most of the early pioneers of psychiatry and psychology placed a decided emphasis on early childhood experiences to the almost total neglect of adult experience. Modern theorists, in seeking a more balanced approach to human development, have conducted more research on the adult years. Generally, their approaches can be categorized as "stage theories" or "age theories."

Stage theorists believe that individuals mature by journeying successfully through predictable crises or stages in their lives.

They use such terms as "milestones" or "markers" and focus on the experiences themselves instead of on the time at which the experiences occur. In clerical or religious life, milestones include acceptance into the religious community, ordination to priesthood, profession of final vows, and the jubilee years. In the development of a lesbian or gay identity, for example, many researchers and writers have posed theories on the stages of the coming out process.

Age theorists, by contrast, consider adult development in terms of time or chronological age instead of adult crises or life phases. They acknowledge that significant experiences occur in the maturation process, but prefer to focus their research on the particular age or time period at which they happen. Daniel Levinson (1978), a popular age theorist, divides adult development into four stages: early (20 to 40 years), middle (40 to 60 years), late (60 to 80 years), and late-late (80 years and over) adulthood.

The events, feelings, and significant changes an individual experiences during the middle years or midlife have often been described as a "midlife crisis." Because the word "crisis" usually denotes a single, discrete event rather than an extended period of time, words such as "transition" or "passage" better characterize what transpires during the many years between early and late adulthood. Many people erroneously believe that a woman's midlife is synonymous with the advent of menopause, a time in which various hormonal changes occur in the woman's body. The fact that these two stages in a woman's life are not identical becomes clear when we consider the ages of occurrence. The average age at which women experience menopause is 50 while the majority of women begin to enter a midlife passage in their late 30's or early 40's. Menopause usually begins at the end rather than at the beginning of the midlife transition.

If menopause is characterized by biological changes, midlife is accompanied by interior, psychological changes. Properly speaking, career changes, bodily aging, difficulties in relationships, and changes in sexual behavior are external symptoms that reflect the midlife transition; they themselves do not constitute the midlife transition. The midlife passage itself is an interior journey into the core of one's being, a retreat into the self. During this extended inner pilgrimage there is a shattering of values, a questioning of traditional beliefs and opinions, a total reassessment of all aspects of life: physical, intellectual, spiritual, emotional, social, vocational. All that seemed so stable and secure in the past begins to crumble and leaves the religious vulnerable and confused. For the lesbian nun, this inner journey involving confusion and uncertainty is very much bound up with the realization and acceptance of her sexual identity.

These middle years can be imaged as a tumultuous and turbulent sea. But gradually a rebuilding of one's philosophical framework emerges as the religious comes to accept and love her newly discovered self. With the passage of time, stability and peace return. Life feels more normal as the religious integrates newly discovered facets of her personality.

The midlife years for women are generally thought to be between 35 and 55, earlier than the 40 to 60 years of age usually ascribed to midlife for males. On average, female children usually learn to walk, speak, read, and write sooner than males. They also enter puberty and midlife at an earlier age than males. Similar to the female population as a whole, most nuns begin their midlife transition between the ages of 35 and 40.

Midlife transition often begins with some precipitating event or change, such as a relocation in residence, a change of job or career, or the illness or death of a loved one. For many lesbian nuns who entered community between the ages of 14 and 18 and who assumed they were heterosexual, this unexpected event of midlife may usher in a decade or more of dealing with the realization of their sexual orientation.

For example, Ruth, a midlife lesbian nun who publicly shared her story at a New Ways Ministry Symposium in 1986, was jolted into this awareness when she saw the film *Personal Best*. Extremely disappointed at the ending of the film, in which a lesbian relationship dissolves when one of the women enters a heterosexual union, Ruth experienced turmoil at the thought that her reactions identified so strongly with the confirmed lesbian character. She began to examine her sheltered life. Her crushes on some special female friends in junior high school did not bother her at the time because she knew that many adolescents had crushes on teachers and friends as an expression of hero worship. But she recalled that she never had any comparable crushes on boys. Living in a small, rural area, Ruth told herself that her selection pool would expand in college.

College, graduate school, and the work environment brought frequent contact with a number of attractive men. She would fantasize about how she would behave should she ever feel romantic attractions to a man, but none of these fantasies ever materialized. She never experienced any erotic desires for men. Then, in her middle years, Ruth began to understand why.

Sheila Murphy (1983), a psychologist who founded and directs the Center for the Study of Counseling Religious, conducted a study of women religious in midlife transition. Murphy drew material for her interviews and questionnaire with 144 women religious from studies of midlife men as well as midlife women because she believed that the lifestyle of nuns contained similarities to the lifestyles of men as well as women. Like midlife women in general, nuns struggled with sexuality and intimacy concerns, but nuns did not deal with problems associated with the "empty nest" syndrome, which consumes so much attention in the literature on midlife women. Because women religious, like midlife men, also pursued careers in a competitive society, she examined research on midlife men that focused on career and family.

My pastoral experience leads me to believe that the results Murphy found about midlife women religious in general parallel the lives of lesbian religious. The difference, of course, for the lesbian religious is that her midlife issues revolve significantly around her discovery, acceptance, and/or integration of her sexual orientation. This chapter will include comments on six of Murphy's findings and show how they relate to the midlife transition of lesbian nuns. These six findings can be categorized as faith-crisis, parent-child relationships, authority issues, career, vocation, and intimacy. The first five will be briefly discussed while more extensive comments will be made on the final topic of intimacy because it affects the lives of lesbian nuns significantly more than the other issues.

Specific Midlife Issues

Murphy found that the majority of women religious in midlife transition experienced some sort of faith crisis. A lesbian nun in her middle years is no exception. More often than not, she experiences a deep crisis of faith because of her sexuality. Feeling lonely, empty, abandoned by the God she faithfully strove to serve, she questions why God made her "this way," why she is "different." She feels an extended period of dryness in prayer. God seems infinitely distant, even completely absent. This "dark night of the soul" flows from the fear and confusion associated with the discovery of her same-sex attractions. This seeming inability to pray will often prompt her to question God's existence. After many years of denial and internalized homophobia surrounding her true feelings, the religious comes to an eventual recognition and claiming of her lesbian identity. Only then does the faith crisis subside. She begins to feel that God truly loves her as the sexual person she is. Describing her own middle years in a book on homosexuality and religious life, Sister Mary (1989) writes, "I can now see what I believe is God's wonderful providence, timing, and planning of the events of my life so that I could be gradually readied to accept myself and my sexual identity more fully" (p. 61).

Although nearly half of the nuns in Murphy's study stated that they had begun to assert independence from their parents before midlife, the overwhelming majority indicated that conflicts and pressures with parents continued into their middle years. They tried to redefine the parent-child relationship as one of parent-adult daughter. The need of the midlife lesbian nun to redefine the parent-child relationship is compounded by the overlay of her sexual orientation. She struggles to be treated as an adult by her parents, and questions whether or not she should reveal her sexual orientation to them. Will they accept or reject her if they know she is lesbian? I know many lesbian nuns in midlife who have shared the knowledge of their orientation with siblings but very few who have informed their parents. Most believe that on some level their parents know they are lesbian but the issue of homosexuality is simply never openly addressed.

In one sense, religious superiors or administrators, as authority figures, may serve *in loco parentis*. Lesbian nuns have been more forthright with these parental figures, but only after years of personal struggle with sexuality and intimacy issues. With rare exceptions these parent figures have been understanding and supportive.

In the Murphy study, the majority of nuns indicated a change in their attitude toward both church and civil authorities, who were respected but not without question. Within religious structures, for example, the opinions and wishes of authority figures were not blindly obeyed as they had once been. These changes, however, are due as much, if not more, to the attitudinal shifts associated with Vatican II and the women's movement in church and society as they are to the onset of midlife.

The midlife lesbian nun experiences great difficulty with institutional church authority because of the church's official condemnation of homogenital behavior and its less than accepting stance on homosexual orientation. In attempting to accept these official views, the lesbian religious feels a crucial component of her own personhood rejected or devalued. She has been taught to feel guilt and shame because of an erotic attraction or love for another woman. Eventually, with the help of therapy, friends, the women's movement, and God's grace, she recognizes the cognitive dissonance between her instinctual belief in the inherent goodness of her own lesbian feelings and the negative position of church authorities. She learns to trust her own experience and to overcome her guilt feelings. Because she interprets the official church condemnation of all homogenital behavior as a rejection of the full personhood of lesbian and gay persons who have not voluntarily chosen a life of perpetual celibacy, the credibility factor of the institutional church dramatically decreases in her estimation.

About three-fourths of the nuns in Murphy's study changed careers during midlife and a majority experienced a vocational crisis and considered leaving the convent. During midlife most lesbian nuns change jobs or careers, which often results in deeper revelations about their sexual selves. Some nuns, like Ann, whom I interviewed many years ago for an article about lesbian nuns, come to a full awareness of their sexual orientation as a result of working for lesbian and gay Catholics. "I wanted to see what I could do to help," she told me. "Then I began to realize that was me. I thought, `In no way do I want this.'" Ann says that she probably had inklings of her orientation years before but no full realization. When she was thirty, Ann was very attracted to a woman and thought she was "so bad" because of these feelings. At various times, strong physical desires for women would overwhelm her but she would panic. "I was afraid of human expressions of love, embracing and things like that, which made me very cold and aloof," she confided to me.

As a girl, Ann never experienced any romantic or sexual attraction to boys. "I played with them, I was a tomboy, I had lots of boyfriends," she recalls. "But no dating whatsoever, no attraction. I should have taken the cue, but I didn't know the difference." Only through her chaplaincy work with Dignity during midlife did Ann come to accept her lesbian identity.

Coming to an awareness of one's sexual orientation often precipitates a vocational crisis. Many women ask, "Are lesbian feelings and religious life compatible?" Usually lesbian nuns conclude that they are but sometimes they choose to leave their communities. This departure from the convent during the middle years is preceded by years of struggling with sexual feelings. There are many lesbian nuns who were loved and respected by peers and religious authorities alike; and they loved their communities. Their stories are all very similar. The sister meets a wonderful woman with whom she can share deeply. She feels renewed and energized by the other woman to pursue her ministry more vigorously. Because it is often not possible to effect a living arrangement with the woman, she makes a painful decision to leave the convent. "In my heart I will always be a sister," the nuns remark. Too many times dedicated lesbian nuns sacrifice their religious vocations because some individuals in religious authority positions are unwilling to allow their members to live with laywomen or with sisters of other congregations.

Intimacy
Perhaps the most interesting facet of Murphy's findings, and one

that affects most forcefully the lives of lesbian nuns, dealt with intimacy issues and needs for meaningful relationships. Although intimacy is often mistakenly equated solely with genitality in popular usage, intimacy includes deep affectivity and sexuality in the broad sense. Because a woman's sexual interest begins to accelerate in her 30's and somewhat later, because a woman loses her sexual inhibitions as she begins to mature, and because she feels added intimacy needs, the midlife woman religious is faced with a serious dilemma. Often lonely, wrestling with vocational doubts, less than fulfilled in her career, she is vulnerable to the experience of falling in love and the power of sexual passion. What often happens is that she falls in love with love, especially if she repressed experiences of infatuation before she entered the convent.

Almost all of the nuns Murphy surveyed reported more intense sexual interest and desire as they entered midlife. More than two-thirds of these women engaged in some form of affectional or physical behavior they considered sexual. The activities ranged from prolonged embracing, to kissing and petting, to genital intercourse. Some reported a single encounter; others, numerous experiences over extended time periods. About half of the nuns indicated that they had a male partner; approximately 20%, a female partner, and 30% reported involvement with a male and a female.

Murphy's results are similar to some findings in a 1981 doctoral dissertation by Ellen Rufft, CDP, who compared "Stages of Adult Development for Women Religious and Married Women" in their midlife experiences. Of the 117 women religious Rufft surveyed, 41% reported some sexual involvement with a man; 39% reported involvement with a woman (Murphy, 1983). Both studies suggest that many, though not all, nuns engage in sexual and affectional behavior in dealing with their intimacy needs during midlife.

We are beginning to learn that it is unrealistic to expect clergy and religious to serve humankind to the neglect of their own needs for emotional and sexual fulfillment. Lesbian religious report that they grow into a proper love of themselves, their community, and their God through deep love relationships with other individuals. Most of the early years in religious life are devoted to a highly professional preparation for ministry to the virtual neglect of personal development. Eventually the heart and the body demand equal time. The search for human intimacy and companionship constitutes a major part of the middle years.

It is very natural for a lesbian woman to fall in love with women who share similar values, goals, and aspirations. Sister Madelyn, another woman who spoke publicly at a New Ways Ministry symposium, claimed that her story was not atypical. While she was in temporary vows, Madelyn was required to meet weekly with Jane, her community leader. At first she rebelled at the obligation of sharing her growth process in prayer, community, and ministry with Jane. But much to Madelyn's surprise, these encounters became a vehicle for recognition and appreciation of the giftedness of the other. What began as drudgery evolved into moments of intense respect, challenge, love, and forgiveness. Through her love relationship with Jane, Madelyn came to understand and accept the depth in which she was loved by God. She counted as sacred those moments of emotional, spiritual, physical, and social sharing.

Madelyn's spiritual director recommended that she decide between religious life and her relationship with Jane. According to him, the two were incompatible. In choosing to end her friendship with Jane, Madelyn also constructed barriers to future relationships and lived a life devoid of human intimacy for many years. Whenever she experienced strong physical attractions, she would sever the relationship. As she said, she had decided to remain a committed celibate religious woman as defined by the "patriarchal church." This advice, together with Madelyn's increasing dissatisfaction with and resentment of the "male church," resulted in a devastating loss for her religious community. Madelyn eventually left the congregation of women, which she still loves to this day.

Celibacy

In conversations with lesbian nuns across the country, I find the midlife religious of the 1990s less willing to accept a traditional definition of celibacy. They claim that a passive acceptance and practice of the kind of celibacy they were taught prevents them from experiencing a healthy sexual development.

In sexual research involving four types of American couples (lesbian, gay male, heterosexually married and heterosexually cohabitating), it was found that lesbian couples experience genital sex less frequently than any other type of couple (Blumstein and Schwartz, 1983). Mostly monogamous, lesbian couples are interested in the non-genital, though sexual and sensual, aspects of a relationship: touching, caressing, kissing, hugging, cuddling. Like heterosexual women, lesbian women find it difficult to separate sex from love and the emotional ties of a relationship. Because many males can apparently have sex apart from love more easily than women, it is understandable that gay men can find a willing sex partner more readily than heterosexual men. Gay men apparently experience more sexual encounters than heterosexual men, lesbian women, or heterosexual women. This research suggests that the human male places more emphasis on genital sex than the female, while she seems to feel satisfied and fulfilled by the emotional and sexual content of interpersonal relationships.

What does all this have to do with celibacy, intimacy, and midlife lesbian nuns? The traditional approach to religious celibacy and intimacy has centered around genitality perhaps because the construction of religious life throughout history has been shaped and molded mainly by men. Celibacy was defined as a total ban on genital expression and a pervasive suspicion of close, intimate relationships because of the genital expression to which they might lead. It came to be equated with a total lack of any kind of sexuality. Questions like "How far can you go"? in expressing human affection are peculiar to the traditional conception of celibacy that insists on a clear line of sexual demarcation and on the rule of genital abstinence to protect the self from bodily intimacy and relating. This understanding of celibacy included warnings about particular friendships, proscriptions against entering another person's room, and injunctions to walk in three's or four's, never two's.

The approach to celibacy that most midlife lesbian nuns were taught views human love as competing with divine love. Celibacy is said to be "for the kingdom." Total love of God, threatened by warm, intimate, human relationships, is safeguarded by social interaction in large groups. Bonds of human attachment are to be discouraged as they would be a hindrance in the pursuit and achievement of personal perfection. Celibacy, in this tradition, frees one in order to devote more time to Christian ministry. Its pragmatic side effect is an accumulation of time that can be used to accomplish more work.

Lesbian religious, particularly those in the middle years, are rejecting this traditional approach to celibacy and intimacy in favor of an alternative interpretation. They believe that celibacy, to be authentically human, must maximize opportunities for developing close, intimate relationships. This conception of celibacy springs from women's strong inclinations for relatedness and connection.

This new, woman-centered construction of celibacy is marked by caring, friendship, and responsibility. Such an understanding of celibacy will ask different kinds of questions: How can I best express my caring and my respect for the other? What bodily expressions of affection are appropriate to and a reflection of the depth of my caring for this particular other? If difficulties or tensions arise in relationships, as they inevitably will, how can these dilemmas be resolved in such a way so as to nourish and care for the persons in relationship? How can I avoid exploitation or unnecessary hurt and express concern and care in relationship?

In this woman-centered perspective of celibacy, friendships are valued more than achievements. These friendships are judged as normal and even necessary to adult moral development. Instead of challenging the religious who is "too friendly" with another, feminist spiritual directors are concerned about the celibacy of someone who appears to have no friends.

A viable ethic for a woman-defined celibacy includes personal integrity, mutuality, cooperation, responsibility, and interdependence rather than fulfillment of an obligation or adherence to a sexual rule. The self and the other are treated with mutual value and worth despite, at times, certain difficulties in personal power. Although friends need time alone to nourish their relationship, this vision of celibacy and intimacy strives to include all. Lesbian nuns in their middle years are beginning to rethink celibacy in these more inclusive and integrating terms.

Summary

In this chapter the discussion of midlife lesbian nuns has been situated in the framework of research on midlife in general and on midlife nuns in particular. In so doing we have seen that the issues that midlife lesbian nuns face are rooted in the same ones that their midlife heterosexual counterparts are experiencing, except that they are compounded by the acceptance and integration of their sexual orientation.

The midlife passage is best described as an interior journey in which there is a complete reappraisal of one's identity and existence in relation to one's physical and spiritual life. For lesbian nuns, midlife often begins with an unexpected event that nudges the religious to deal, rather unwillingly at first, with her sexual orientation. This inner work usually involves six main areas: a faith crisis, parent-child relationships, authority issues, career, vocation, and intimacy. This last area is most crucial to lesbian midlife religious.

The need for human intimacy results in social, emotional, spiritual, and sexual bonds that lesbian nuns develop during the middle years. Two previous studies indicated that many nuns engage in sexual and affectional behavior with women as well as with men in dealing with their intimacy needs during midlife. A crisis in the realm of intimate expression is more unsettling for the lesbian religious than for a lay woman or heterosexual nun because the lesbian religious experiences a double stress. Traditionally she was taught to respect celibacy and church teaching regarding homosexual expression. Both values are being challenged during midlife. In the prolonged search for intimacy, most lesbian nuns have found the traditional approach to celibacy and sexuality less than helpful and are rejecting it in favor of an alternative model based on caring and loving relationships in a community context.

–10–

U.S. Bishops
and Current Thinking

At their November 1990 meeting the Catholic bishops of the United States overwhelmingly approved a document entitled *Human Sexuality: A Catholic Perspective for Education and Lifelong Learning*. It contains a section on homosexuality. The last time the bishops addressed this controversial topic was in their 1976 pastoral letter on moral values where they devoted one brief, but mostly positive, paragraph to it. Some of their observations at that time on justice, respect, and pastoral care for gay and lesbian people have been incorporated into the new statement.

In 1986 the Vatican helped fuel the discussion with a letter to the bishops of the world on the pastoral care of homosexual people issued by the Congregation for the Doctrine of the Faith. The letter provoked strong reactions from the theological and lesbian and gay communities both in the United States and abroad. One of the major struggles at the bishops' meeting was over the value of the Vatican document's description of the homosexual orientation as a "disorder." The discussion as well as the document's final wording indicates that, since their first public pronouncement in 1976, the bishops have learned much about homosexuality and the tensions it causes in the church.

The major treatment of the subject in *Human Sexuality* is found in Chapter 4, "Special Groups and Sexual Issues: Moral Discernment and Pastoral Care." For a fuller understanding of the bishops' approach to homosexuality, this section ought to be read in conjunction with the previous chapters which lay the foundation for Catholic sexual teaching. The subsection "Persons With a Homosexual Orientation" consists of eight paragraphs documented by ten references. Four references allude to the bishops' own 1976 pastoral on moral values and three to the 1986 Vatican letter. The three other sources are a guide to confessors published by a committee of the National Conference of Catholic Bishops in 1973, the *Declaration on Certain Questions Concerning Sexual Ethics* issued by the Congregation for the Doctrine of the Faith in 1976 and the Congregation for Catholic Education's own sex education guidelines of 1983.

The American bishops' discussion of homosexuality begins with a repetition of their strong conviction that sexuality is a fundamental dimension of every human being which has implications for the physical, psycho-emotional, intellectual, spiritual, ethical, and social facets of the human personality. In Chapter 2 they state explicitly that not only married people, but also "homosexual men and women," along with single adults, the divorced and widowed, infants, children and adolescents, are sexual beings and experience their sexuality "in a variety of ways." They seem to understand the difference between gender identity (who I am as a male or female), sexual orientation (whom I am attracted to), and sexual behavior. Their definition of a homosexual orientation rightly places the emphasis on the attraction to persons of the same sex rather than to particular sex acts.

Call for Respect

The bishops counter the common myth that people choose to be homosexual (and, therefore, can also choose not to be) by acknowledging that for some young people homosexuality is a "discovery." Reflecting a 1976 Vatican statement on sexual ethics, which was the first official church document to acknowledge the distinction between orientation and behavior, they differentiate "transitory" homosexuality from a "permanent, seemingly irreversible sexual orientation." Their use of the word "orientation" rather than "tendencies," "condition," or "inclination" represents the best current opinion of the sciences. One bishop did suggest that the word "attraction" be submitted for "orientation," since many scientists think of homosexuality merely as a stage of development, whereas the document presents homosexual orientation "as a simple fact." However, the committee rejected the introduction of a new term. The bishops, obviously cognizant of the complex and inconclusive scientific discourse on the aetiology of homosexuality, prudently avoided taking any position on the causes of homosexuality and refer only in passing to some of the more substantive theories.

Moving quickly to other ground on which they feel more secure, they repeat the strong call they themselves made in 1976 for respect, justice, and friendship for gay and lesbian people. Rather cleverly, they support their assertion with a direct reference to one of the few sections of the 1986 Vatican letter that won any significant praise. That section stated that "violent malice in speech and action" directed against homosexual people deserves "condemnation from the church's pastors wherever it occurs."

The original draft of the bishops' document called on Christians to confront and curb "homophobic" fears, jokes, and discrimination. An amendment to this section from the National Advisory Council composed of lay, clerical, and religious representatives suggested a change in the wording that eliminated the word "homophobia." The final draft reads, "We call on all Christians of good will to confront their own fears about homosexuality and to curb the humor and discrimination that offends homosexual persons." Objections could be made to the ambivalence of the word "curb," as opposed to the much stronger "eliminate," for many of the same reasons that bishops objected to its use in their statement on production of nuclear weapons.

The reality of homophobia and its impact on social and church life are becoming increasingly more understood in the light of the documented rise in violence, victimization, and defamation experienced by gay and lesbian people. Current studies suggest that as much as 17% of this violence is perpetrated out of motives related to AIDS. It would have strengthened the bishops' position considerably to have used the term "homophobia." It is probably not unfair to suggest that few of them are sufficiently aware of the studies and data on the dynamics of this phenomenon. On the level of personal experience many of them are undoubtedly aware of the debilitating effects of homophobia in the lives of men and women they know. Some are conscious of their own homophobia and its effects on the institution; a few, seemingly, are not.

When the bishops addressed homogenital behavior, they did so by referring to their own carefully worded 1976 judgment that homosexual activity is "morally wrong" because it is genital sexual activity outside marriage. For the Christian tradition, only in marriage is genital sexuality morally acceptable. It was at this point that some bishops were not content to merely distinguish homosexual orientation from homosexual behavior.

Thus Bishop Raymond Lessard of Savannah proposed an amendment that included the language of the Congregation for the Doctrine of the Faith describing the "inclination" of the homosexual person as an "objective disorder." Several bishops spoke against this amendment. Michael Kenny of Alaska said that it will "only further alienate a community already alienated and hurt." San Francisco's John Quinn argued that it would be misinterpreted to mean that "homosexual people are evil" and Hartford's Peter Rosazza said it would be "offensive" to them. Quinn also pointed out that the word "disorder" is a philosophical description bound to be misunderstood in the press and suggested that something be added to the text to indicate that homosexuals are not unique; all of us have disordered tendencies.

Boston's Cardinal Bernard Law supported the amendment because, he said, the church has no choice but to "teach the whole truth." When the retired Archbishop of Baltimore, William Borders, said the purpose of any pastoral statement was to help people and not cause more pain, Francis DiLorenzo of Scranton, Pennsylvania, countered that the document's only aim was to provide guidelines containing "the irreducible minimum" for diocesan leaders and that these were "a reservoir of correct doctrine, not a response to pastoral problems."

Cardinal Joseph Bernardin, Archbishop of Chicago, the bishops' great reconciler, wanted both to support the Congregation for the Doctrine of the Faith and to be sensitive to the legitimate concerns of lesbian and gay people. He offered a compromise allowing the initial wording to remain unchanged but adding an explanatory footnote. When Bishop Lessard declined to withdraw his original amendment, even though he was aware of the pastoral problems involved in presenting "the full truth" of Catholic teaching on homosexuality by the use of the term "disorder," the question was called and the amendment was defeated.

Bernardin then suggested adding a description of the orientation as not sinful because not freely chosen and including the language of the Congregation for the Doctrine of the Faith in a footnote. Archbishop Quinn continued to insist that some clarification be included to explain that the use of the word "disorder" is not the same as calling a gay or lesbian person evil. One bishop wanted to say the orientation is not sinful "when" it is not chosen rather than "because" it is not chosen, but Archbishop Oscar Lipscomb of Mobile pointed out that one "can never freely choose an orientation" whereas the use of "when" would imply that one could.

In speaking of pastoral care for homosexual people, the bishops repeat a statement of the 1976 Vatican declaration that homosexual men and women "must certainly be treated with understanding" and "sustained in Christian hope." For many interpreters the "hope" is a hope that the church will eventually accept gay and lesbian people fully, including their responsible genital relationships. Obviously the bishops did not intend that interpretation. Nevertheless, they chose to omit the second part of that Vatican statement which describes the "hope" as "overcoming their personal difficulties and their inability to fit into society."

Following traditional theological principles, the bishops say that the moral responsibility of homosexual people, presumably for their own sexual behavior, ought to be judged "with a degree of prudence." The same approach is applied to other sexual issues in an earlier section on theological principles, which states that "the process of moving from absolute values to general norms to specific case judgments requires the virtue of prudence." One implication is that in some instances people might not always be subjectively guilty for objectively wrong behavior.

More pertinent to the lives of the majority of gay and lesbian Catholics today is the bishops' acknowledgment that ultimately each person "must discern his or her own moral decisions and wider vocational calling." Quoting Vatican II, the bishops say that "conscience is the most secret core and sanctuary of a person." Such decisions apply to the single or the married, widowed or divorced or celibate people. For some reason, whether deliberate or not, "homosexual people" are omitted from the list, but the bishops cannot mean that these same decisions do not apply in their case.

A Complex Issue

Not surprisingly, the bishops advise chastity for gay and lesbian people. Elsewhere in the document, however, they make a statement about chastity that could be applied analogously to gay and lesbian people. Chastity, they say, "is not synonymous with an interior calling to perpetual celibacy." Strictly speaking, the church requires chastity of all single people including gay and lesbian Catholics. Although the chaste single state excludes genital intimacy, it does not rule out a committed, bonded relationship and the sharing of life and love with another person. Some official Catholic documents on homosexuality have already argued that stable, faithful, committed but chaste homosexual relationships are not outside valid pastoral possibilities and characterized them as a better moral situation than promiscuity.

Catholic teaching, then, can already be seen as supportive of homosexual, committed relationships that exclude genitality. Still the bishops are realistic enough to realize that relationships between unmarried heterosexual couples will tend to include physical expression. In speaking of cohabitation among heterosexual couples, the document acknowledges that such an arrangement does not necessarily involve genital sexual intimacy, but "it does establish a situation in which avoidance of non-marital sex becomes exceptionally difficult, particularly for those couples bound by affection." The bishops of England and Wales anticipated this situation when they offered pastoral guidelines in 1979. They advised pastors to distinguish between "irresponsible, indiscriminate sexual activity and the permanent association between two homosexual persons who feel incapable of enduring a solitary life devoid of sexual expression" (Catholic Social Welfare Commission, 1981, p. 8). They refused, however, to compare this situation analogously with the marriage relationship as objectively good.

In a brief section on education about homosexuality, the bishops assert that the topic cannot be avoided. Teaching must include respect for people regardless of sexual orientation. The unambiguous moral norms of the Christian tradition must be presented "clearly and delicately." They state that there should be a supportive approach based on the realization that "some students will be struggling to accept their homosexuality."

The bishops refer to the distinction between orientation and behavior as "being" homosexual and "doing" homosexual actions. They honestly acknowledge that the difference is "not always clear and convincing." They are undoubtedly aware that while many people find the distinction useful in teaching and counselling programs on homosexuality, they do not find it particularly helpful in the pastoral field or fully congruent with the experiences of gay and lesbian Catholics. It has been challenged on both philosophical and psychological grounds. Richard Sipe (1990) is correct when he says that we need to abandon "the simplistic assumption that the distinction...is sufficient to define accurately the reality" (p. 104).

The bishops' most recent treatment of homosexuality is far

more extensive than their attempt in 1976 and, on the whole, still more positive, nuanced, and supportive than many other statements coming from official sources. It does not offer any major breakthroughs in the official understanding of homosexuality, nor does it attempt to address any of the claims of the revisionist theologians. It does, however, show development in the bishops' appreciation of the complexity of the issue and the need for accuracy and sensitivity when presenting the church's position.

–11–

Theological Contributions of the U.S. Church

In this chapter I would like to discuss the contributions on the topic of homosexuality that have emerged from the U.S. theological community and from gay and lesbian Catholics themselves. The majority of mainstream U.S. moral theologians, with guarded support from some episcopal leaders, have applied traditional theological principles to concrete pastoral situations of gay and lesbian Catholics. However, more radical development, in the form of new paradigms or ways of viewing human sexuality, is being articulated by a minority of Catholic theologians and confirmed by the lived experience of the majority of gay and lesbi-

an people. The theological developments center around evaluations of the homosexual orientation and homogenital acts.

Homosexual Orientation

One of the fundamental questions in the discussion of the homosexual orientation is whether or not the orientation can be
described as humanly normative. Most moralists, drawing on
sources such as Scripture, tradition, and natural law for a definition of the essentially human, believe that it cannot. The approach
to the concept of homosexual orientation taken by Lisa Sowle
Cahill, a moral theologian at Boston College, is illustrative of the
position of these moralists.

Cahill believes that both the consistency and frequency of
homosexuality as a human phenomenon have implications for
moral judgments. Neither is sufficient, she believes, to establish
whether a certain human constitution or behavior is psychologically healthy or pathological, much less whether it is morally
right or wrong. According to Cahill (1985a), "if certain biological or
psychological conditions constantly recur in human societies, then
the members of those societies have the obligation to enhance
human life as far as possible in the midst of those conditions,
whether the conditions themselves are desirable or undesirable"
(p. 147). For Cahill, the final normative judgment is that a homosexual orientation is "less than fully human," although she
honestly admits that in reaching this conclusion, the use of both
biblical and non-biblical sources "is not beyond equivocation"
(Cahill, 1983, p. 88). The solution for her is to distinguish carefully
between: 1) normative evaluations of the homosexual orientation,
2) evaluations of the concrete justifiability of homosexual acts in
specific circumstances, and 3) the moral character and potential of
homosexual persons.

It is in Cahill's first point that the discussion can be moved.

This can be done by considering the results of empirical studies, by a careful examination of recent writings on natural law, and by some further explication of the objective norms of Christian morality proposed by Vatican II. The *Pastoral Constitution on the Church in the Modern World* speaks of "objective standards...based on the nature of the human person and his acts" (Abbott, 1966, p. 256). This is not to imply, as Cahill reminds us, that the Council documents in any way deny the reality of a common human nature or of a human universal morality known by reason. But they do highlight the importance of realizing "that 'human nature,' that is, human experience, is historical, particular, relational and diverse" (Cahill, 1985a, p. 497).

The *Pastoral Constitution on the Church in the Modern World* also says that "the human race has passed from a rather static concept of reality to a more dynamic, evolutionary one" (Abbott, 1966, p. 204). Ethics has come to be seen more in reaction to the person in the concrete than to human nature in the abstract. The document from the Senate of Priests (1983) of the Archdiocese of San Francisco, speaking of the experiences of many gay and lesbian Christians, says that one of their worst burdens is being outwardly taboo in society and religious circles, "while inwardly sensing a rightness about their sexuality" (p. 8).

Cahill's second point of justifying homosexual acts in specific circumstances runs into difficulties with the magisterial teaching that there can be no justification under any circumstances. Her third point regarding the moral character of homosexual persons is commonly accepted teaching, though very new, and probably not yet even familiar to the majority of Catholic people in our parishes today.

While some theologians like Cahill might be willing to assert that what is humanly nonnormative is not necessarily immoral, for many others this still does not address the crucial theological question. David Kelsey (1984), a Protestant ethicist, asks if there is anything about Christian faith and life...that obliges...[us] to claim that heterosexuality is a timelessly unchanging structure of human nature that the Creator intends as part of human fulfillment" (p. 11). Is it essential to stress historicity in a Christian view of what is normative for humanity? Because until the middle of the twentieth century society stated that heterosexuality was necessary to be fully human, should Christianity accept this historical judgment?

Recently there have been some small indications that point to newer directions in this area. Some voices are beginning to suggest that the homosexual orientation as part of human sexuality might be judged as a positive moral good and central to one's relationship to God and to others. Human sexuality as a condition is never morally neutral but can be a moral good especially as a channel to other values such as intimacy, friendship, and trust. A homosexual orientation can be valued as a building block for one's life. Coleman (1984) states, "For true homosexuals, no amount of will power and no amount of spirituality can alter the fact that they are erotically attracted by members of their own sex" (p. 13). Where might these new directions lead?

From one perspective, the fundamental issue is the psychological or philosophical judgment of the homosexual identity and the moral and ethical implications of that judgment. When the natural sciences and some church documents do not treat the homosexual orientation as flawed, the path seems clear for a kinder judgment; namely, that a homosexual identity is a variant form of human psychosexual development within the range of healthy psychological functioning. In this understanding humanity is not thought of as an unchangeable creation of a past accomplishment, but rather as a life to which we have been summoned as a future promise.

But the theological question remains. If human sexual identity is part of the good of creation and a part of the giftedness of each person, and if the homosexual identity is one way that a seemingly consistent percentage of people develop that is well within the norm of healthy human sexuality, then can the physical embodiment of this particular form of sexual identity be acknowledged and affirmed?

Homogenital Acts

The second theological development involves the application of the traditional objective-subjective distinction in the moral evaluation of sexual behavior. Classical church teaching has always recognized that certain acts are judged objectively immoral and generally to be avoided because they involve some kind of harm for the individual and/or others in and of themselves apart from the intentions, results, or circumstances involved. However, responsibility or guilt for these acts can be increased, diminished, or even eliminated completely by certain subjective and personal factors.

This distinction has been traditionally employed in the context of sacramental confession or pastoral counseling. The *Declaration on Sexual Ethics* from the Vatican's Congregation for the Doctrine of the Faith (1976) recognizes this when it says, "Their culpability will be judged with prudence" (par. 8). The degree of subjective culpability for a particular immoral act is distinguished from the objective badness of the act itself.

Richard McCormick has argued for an understanding of this distinction that involves not only the personal, subjective responsibility for the act, but also the objective nature of the act itself. In his book *The Critical Calling*, which contains his most extensive treatment of the topic, McCormick (1989) makes a careful analysis of the implications of the nuanced approach to homogenital acts first articulated by the Catholic bishops of England and Wales.

McCormick argues that we must consider the meaning and pattern of homosexual acts in a person's life. There are circumstances that can affect our judgments when we apply to individuals the moral norm that says these acts should be avoided. When we do this, it affects the very meaning of the objective act itself. This may mean that we can judge the person not culpable subjectively, and in some cases the objective act itself may be judged to be not morally wrong. McCormick believes that the concrete application of the general objective norm about the morality of homogenital acts to a particular situation can qualify or even suspend the moral norm, depending on how completely that norm is formulated in the first place.

McCormick amplifies on the English bishops' contention that "the goodness or badness of an act can only be judged morally in practice when consideration has been given to intention and circumstances" (Catholic Social Welfare Commission, 1981, p. 9). He says that one could objectively justify homogenital acts while still holding to the general norm. The English bishops give as an example the case of an individual who argues that the stability of a particular homosexual union outweighs the disorder of the homosexual acts that take place within it.

Moral theologians, such as Philip Keane (1977), who support the above approach still hold the heterosexual norm and ascribe to homosexual unions a certain disvalue, ontic or pre-moral evil, a lack of vocational integrity, or even some kind of flaw. They are willing nevertheless to justify them in certain circumstances. Curran (1983) sees them as objectively morally good even though he bases his position on the "presence of the sin of the world" (p. 162). Curran refers to "the power of sin in the world," which justifies certain acts not justified in an ideal situation. McCormick also refers to "the power of sin" in relation to a "deviation of instinct" not in one's control. Other more traditional moralists like Notre Dame's Edward Malloy (1981) and James Hanigan (1988) are only willing to tolerate homosexual unions as a lesser evil than promiscuity.

McCormick and others attempting to renew Roman Catholic morality believe that morality is too often equated with acts, especially external ones. For them morality is also concerned with the meaning of our actions. In the area of sexual morality especially, meaning and morality have been seen too exclusively in terms of acts. Sexuality is a basic capacity for relatedness and sexual acts are the language of relationship. But relationships can be exploitative, selfish, and destructive and so can the sexual language employed. These theologians are willing to expand the meaning of sexuality to include relatedness, self-disclosure in sexual acts, and even fecundity beyond strictly biological life. But most of them are unwilling to abandon completely, as without any ethical consequences, the given biological and psychological structures of the fundamental male-female distinction as it affects human relationships, especially sexual ones.

Some theologians are exploring other paradigms that view human sexuality as primarily relational and less tied to anatomical structures. Xavier Seubert (1991), a sacramental theologian, explored this approach at a Notre Dame conference on AIDS and in a subsequent article. He employed the Broadway play *M. Butterfly* to illustrate how we can "open up" traditional paradigms of sexuality with new impulses about sexual and gender roles, some of which come from the experiences of gay and lesbian people. Seubert notes that the central and foundational image of the Creator is a traditional community of love called the Trinity. The image is cast as a relationship between the Father and the Son with the Spirit of love that flows from them. This is a more primary image for Christians than the image of God in Genesis. The flow of life among us, for Seubert, does not depend simply on literal, biological complementarity. The traditional image of the Trinity, in which there is no gender complementarity, can be a warning against considering the human and biological complementarity of the sexes to be the natural culmination of our being made in the "image and likeness" of God. Complementarity is necessary for procreation. It might not be necessary for the level of exchange of life in relationships.

The discussion thus far has focused primarily on the theological formulations of Cahill and McCormick as representative of the moderate opinions of the majority of U.S. moral theologians today. An excellent treatment of both the moderate and progressive stances of most of the U.S. theological community regarding homogenital expression can be found in the study on sexuality commissioned by the Catholic Theological Society of America (Kosnik, Carroll, Cunningham, Modras, and Schulte, 1977). Not yet discussed is the position of a minority of U.S. moral theologians who support the church ban on all homogenital behavior in any context. Chapter 13 contains a critique of the work of James Hanigan, whose exposition and defense of the traditional teaching represents the most creative approach of this group.

New Models From Gay and Lesbian Experiences
Some theologians and gay and lesbian Catholics are willing to take a further step in challenging the heterosexual norm. Their principal spokespersons have been some Roman Catholic feminist theologians (Farley, 1983; Ruether, 1989), a few Catholic male theologians (McNeill, 1976; Maguire, 1983) and in a less systematic and more experiential way, the vast majority of gay and lesbian Catholic activists. A discussion of the views of these more progressive theologians can be found in Chapter 12.

The basic question gay and lesbian Catholics raise is this: why is heterosexuality judged to be normative for full humanity and sexuality? What are the grounds for such a claim? Do we need to examine that claim and all of its sources, including biblical, psychological, and theological ones? Is heterosexuality such an intrinsic part of authentic human nature that without it the individual person is in some way lacking or inferior? Is human nature the same for all times or are we learning more and more about previous positions concerning what is normative? Do we not need to be a bit more humble about definite teachings on sexuality in the face of new information from the sciences, as Rembert Weakland (1980) has suggested?

Many believe that homosexuality has not yet been imagined as a possibility for authentic humanity and Christian living. Part of the difficulty, according to Seubert, is that the metaphorical process for thinking about homosexuality with its own powers and possibilities for human living has been stopped. Gay and lesbian Christians are calling upon the broader church to look with them at their experience of the truth of their sexual reality because the sexual norms we have are not informed by their experience. The core experience of a human person should elicit respect and attention; otherwise real understanding remains superficial at best and harmful at worst. Seubert (1991) says, "Until the homosexual experience is truthfully spoken and truthfully heard, the disorder will not be homosexuality, but the inability of the church to stand in truth, endure it and live from it" (pp. 62-63).

Seubert contends that new aspects of the metaphor of church as sacrament are being fashioned by gay and lesbian experience. Their whole lives are graced and sacramental because of their sexuality. This experience does not diminish in the face of negative statements and action by church authorities, but seems to grow in conviction. Gay and lesbian Catholics by and large in the U.S.

have chosen to remain uneasily at times within the church (Grippo, 1990). They cannot simply turn away from the church even when its statements have not adequately addressed what they experience to be a fundamental part of their lives.

Of all the resources we use in responding to the complexities of homosexuality the personal testimony and experience of gay and lesbian Catholics is the least developed. Yet it can be argued that it is the most valuable contribution the U.S. Catholic community can make to the theological reflection on homosexuality and to the continued development of homosexuality as a pastoral issue facing the church. Personal experience alone, however, is never adequate for definitive ethical and moral judgments until tested against other sources in the tradition. But if its voice is not even heard as part of the whole process, then principles of sexual ethics, pastoral advice, and theological developments will be impoverished and ultimately discredited for increasing numbers of people.

The gay and lesbian Catholic experience has come primarily from a select and limited portion of gay and lesbian Catholics associated with Dignity. They have offered their personal experiences in such projects as a pastoral letter to the Catholic community and their document on sexual ethics. Other lesbian and gay Catholics have shared their personal stories in books and anthologies (Curb and Manahan, 1985; Gramick, 1983; Gramick, 1989; McNaught, 1988; Wolf, 1989; Zanotti, 1986). These modest but timely contributions reflect a theological shift from a deductive to an empirical method. It remains for the theological community to affirm these attempts, utilize the resources, and personally encourage ongoing reflection and dialogue by all concerned.

The freedom of moral theologians to move in this direction, however, could be seriously threatened by direct outside interventions and attempts to curtail certain trends in moral theology.

But there is little to prevent lay Catholics, other than discouragement and frustration, from continuing to reflect upon their experiences, articulate the goodness and humanity of their lives, and continue to stand in their own truth. In the long run, this might be the most crucial and effective ongoing contribution to the process of analyzing new data, asking new questions, and proposing new answers to questions about homosexuality in particular and sexuality in general.

–12–

The U.S. Church
and Global Significance

Not until the latter half of the twentieth century, and particularly since 1969, have there been any significant developments in the Catholic church's pastoral outreach to lesbian and gay people and any theological rethinking of classical positions on homosexuality. In this chapter, we will see that the U.S. church has advanced this issue globally more than any other national Catholic body, we will analyze why this is so, and demonstrate the significance of these developments for the U.S. church, for the Vatican, and for lesbian and gay Catholics.

Global Contrasts
To appreciate the fact that the U.S. church has developed the issue

of homosexuality more significantly than the church in other parts of the world, we need to examine the global situation. Other national churches in the Catholic community first addressed the issue of homosexuality in 1979. In that year the bishops of England and Wales, through its Catholic Social Welfare Commission (1981), published a set of guidelines for their clergy entitled *An Introduction to the Pastoral Care of Homosexual People*. The main thrust of the document was to dispel stereotypes, to condemn prejudice, and to enable the clergy to deal more sensitively with lesbian and gay persons.

Predictably, the guidelines reaffirmed the church's official teaching that homogenital activity is objectively wrong, although it noted that pastoral distinctions could be made between irresponsible sexual activity and the situation of same-sex, committed couples. In determining whether or not to allow lesbian and gay persons to receive the Eucharist or absolution in the sacrament of Reconciliation, the document stated that "an invincible doubt, whether of law or fact, permits one to follow a true and solidly 'probable opinion' in favor of a more liberal interpretation" (p. 13). These statements were interpreted by many commentators to mean that lesbian and gay Catholics in stable relationships can receive Communion. Although the guidelines attempted to put a more human face on the traditional ban against homogenital activity, they were not widely circulated among the clergy and were met with some displeasure from the Congregation for the Doctrine of the Faith. Thus their potential benefit was greatly blunted.

In August 1979, with the approval of the bishops of the Netherlands, the Catholic Council for Church and Society (1980), an official church agency, published a discussion document for grassroots communities entitled *Homosexual People in Society*. The document strongly rejected biblical appeals to justify prejudice and social discrimination against lesbian and gay people as "an abuse of Scripture" since the biblical authors "were not aware of a constitutional or irreversible homosexual orientation" (p. 15). It asserted that accepting the homosexual orientation, while rejecting the behavior that flows from it, is not an adequate solution. The document asked how an appeal to traditional natural law arguments could be convincing when homogenital behavior is "understood and experienced as a natural expression of a homosexual orientation" (p. 16). It concluded that the church will need to find "stronger arguments, if any exist" (p. 18).

Although lesbian and gay Catholics welcomed the statement from the bishops of the Netherlands more than its British counterpart because of its more direct challenge to the official condemnation of homogenital acts, it seems to have suffered the same fate. The bishops of the Netherlands were summoned to the Vatican for a special pastoral council meeting with Pope John Paul II in 1980, after which they publicly declared their loyalty to the Holy See. *Homosexual People in Society* did not receive the wide circulation and public discussion the authors intended. Like the British guidelines, the Dutch document was probably more widely read and discussed in the United States after New Ways Ministry translated and published an English version of it. In a preface to the U.S. edition, Gregory Baum calls the statement "a remote, hardly audible sign that a change is in the making in the Catholic Church" (p. 4).

The Irish Hierarchy (1985) published a pastoral letter on sexual ethics entitled *Love Is for Life*. In the 115-page document, paragraphs 123-126, which deal with homosexuality, reveal little knowledge of the findings of contemporary science, other than the now familiar distinction between orientation and behavior. The document, in fact, betrays a lack of awareness of the development of a homosexual orientation and merely reinforces some of the worst stereotypes that have been leveled against lesbian and gay persons. It reaffirms the traditional ban on homogenital activity and offers cautious support for campaigns to outlaw social discrimination against lesbian and gay persons.

In October 1986 the New Zealand Catholic Bishops' Conference (1986) published a statement entitled *Dignity, Love, Life* in the form of a letter to Catholic educational, social, and pastoral leaders of their country. Public debates on homosexual law reform occasioned the letter, although some bishops in New Zealand had been publicly celebrating Mass for gay and lesbian Catholics in the Gay Centre several years earlier. In their public statement the bishops are on record as opposing all forms of unjust discrimination against lesbian and gay persons. Making a clear distinction between the legality and the morality of homosexual activity, they note the widespread but erroneous assumption that what is legally permissible is construed as morally acceptable. At the center of this very pastoral letter is an appeal to treat lesbian and gay persons with dignity and respect for their inherent and essential equality with heterosexuals.

The only other national body of bishops, besides those of the Netherlands, England and Wales, Ireland and New Zealand, to address the question of homosexuality, is the U.S. National Conference of Catholic Bishops. Six years prior to the English and Dutch statements, twelve years prior to the Irish pastoral letter, and thirteen years before the New Zealand statement, the U.S. bishops published a booklet setting forth principles to guide confessors in the area of homosexuality. The tone of this document was similar to the quality of the Irish Bishops' letter.

Only three years later, the U.S. bishops took a more compassionate stance when they issued on November 11, 1976, their pastoral letter on moral values, *To Live in Christ Jesus.* Although only one paragraph of the entire pastoral letter dealt with homosexuality, that paragraph seems to have had a wider and more lasting effect than the longer documents from the other national churches. The paragraph contained the outline for expanding the church's theological teaching on homosexuality from a concern merely with orientation and behavior to an added interest in pastoral ministry, human and civil rights, and homophobia or prejudice. The paragraph has been quoted consistently by numerous Catholic treatments of the topic, and even by the New Zealand bishops, as a basis for outreach and ministry to lesbian and gay persons.

Since 1976, more than a dozen U.S. bishops and three State Conferences have addressed the subject (Gallagher, 1986). Some of these episcopal statements reflect a grasp of contemporary social science and biblical interpretations whereas others are filled with myths and misinformation about the social and psychological conditions of lesbian and gay persons. Whatever their quality, these writings have been more extensive and have impacted more individuals and groups than those coming from the bishops of the Netherlands, England and Wales, Ireland, or New Zealand. These assertions are based on knowledge gained from our fact finding trips to Western Europe and from our grassroots contacts with Catholic lesbian and gay leaders across the world.

The controversial 1986 letter from the Congregation for the Doctrine of the Faith reinforced the prominence of the U.S. church in this area by motivating many U.S. bishops to establish public, diocesan-sponsored ministries to lesbian and gay Catholics. Following the Vatican letter, many bishops felt obliged to evict Dignity from the Catholic facilities in their dioceses because the organization opposes official church teaching on homogenital behavior. Most of the diocesan ministries that resulted are similar to Dignity in regard to the clergy who serve the groups, the individuals who participate, and the approach to ministry that is employed. The difference is in the public articulation of the official stance banning homogenital behavior and in the ability of the diocese to exercise control over proposed actions of the group. These diocesan ministries are found in such cities as Seattle, Chicago, and Buffalo, among others. Not all diocesan ministries accept the dominant viewpoint of contemporary psychologists in evaluating a homosexual orientation as a natural variant of sexuality. Some, such as those in New York City and Boston, model themselves on Courage, an organization that views homosexuality as a compulsive disorder.

Thus far, the contention that the U.S. church has advanced the issue of homosexuality more than any other national Catholic body, has been based on the following reasons: 1) the first time Church teachings about homosexuality were articulated in the twentieth century was in the United States, and 2) these teachings have been more substantially developed and far reaching in scope and magnitude than those of other hierarchies, and 3) numerous U.S. dioceses have established lesbian and gay ministries.

Theological Challenge

A fourth factor that accounts for the leadership that the U.S. church has exercised in this area is theological development. Although the worldwide lesbian and gay movement has adopted the Greek letter lambda (λ) to represent their struggle for liberation, no Latin American liberation theologian has yet written explicitly on the topic of lesbian and gay liberation. Theological discussions on homosexuality are not that plentiful even in Europe, although some theologians such as Theo Beemer from the University of Nijmegen and the Redemptorist Ralph Gallagher (1979) in Ireland explored the topic in professional journals in the 1970s. In North America we see the most innovative critiques of the teaching on homogenital activity with the Canadians Gregory Baum (1974) and André Guindon (1986, 1988) and with a host of U.S. moral theologians.

A survey of theological literature on the moral evaluation of homosexuality shows that the contributions from the U.S. Catholic theological community have been the broadest in scope and the most challenging in content. The moderate stance of most U.S. moral theologians regarding homogenital expression has been amply discussed in Chapter 11. This chapter will describe several explorations of a minority of U.S. moral theologians who hold that lesbian and gay persons are a vital part of the Creator's plan for humanity.

The first major challenge to traditional teaching came with John McNeill's (1976) landmark book, *The Church and the Homosexual.* McNeill argues that the human person can be understood in terms of radical freedom. If this is so, the basic moral norm for sexual expression is not connected to procreation but rests on love. For McNeill, the concept of love includes mutuality, fidelity, and unselfishness. Expressions that are loving sexual acts are moral; those lacking in the qualities of love are not. Since lesbian and gay persons are capable of unselfish loving, there is no reason to deny them physical expressions of love, McNeill says.

Margaret Farley (1983) argues that same-sex behavior can be moral providing it meets certain criteria that heterosexual behavior must also fulfill in order to be considered ethical. Farley's ethical norms for sexual expression include: respect for the autonomy of persons, which implies there must be free consent; some degree of mutuality of participation, including mutuality of desire, action, and response; equality of power, which means the absence of domination/subordination roles; some type of commitment, in the sense of providing some form of continued nurturance; fruitfulness that is not closed in on itself but open to nourishing other relationships and to providing service to the wider community. Farley notes that society and the church must address the problem of lack of institutional supports for lesbian and gay people to achieve such ethical relationships.

Daniel Maguire's rejection of what he characterizes as the "be-but-don't-do" theology of the hierarchical magisterium rests simply on justice. Maguire (1983) contends that it is "arbitrary, harmful, cruel, and therefore sinful" (p. 120) to exclude systematically an entire category of people from genital intimacy. He believes that "the marital good of exclusive, committed, enduring, generous, and faithful love is a human good. We have no moral right to declare it off limits to persons whom God has made gay" (p. 133). He says the traditional opposition to homosexual intimacy is based on a "macho-masculine conception of what sex is and how it functions in human personal development" (p. 120).

The progressive theologians have essentially dealt with the two traditional arguments on which the condemnation of homogenital acts is based: procreation and complementarity of the sexes. The love-relational purpose of sex, they say, does not depend on procreation for its justification. If sterile heterosexual couples can express their love genitally with the ecclesial blessing of the institution, and if sex after menopause and the rhythm method are acceptable, then there already is an allowance for some forms of non-procreative sex. These theologians assert that the church is guilty of a double standard by disallowing the love expression of same-sex couples. Maguire (1983) observes that the male-female coital fit and the relationship of heterosexual intercourse to human reproduction are biological facts. "The biologistic error," he states, is to "lead from those facts to the moral imperative that all sexual exchange must be male-female coital in kind." Such a leap, he contends, can be made only if human sexuality is reduced to a "stud farm" mentality (p. 119).

Along with other feminist theologians, Rosemary Ruether (1989) maintains that any condemnation of homogenital acts based on the notion of the complementarity of the sexes is a reinforcement of heterosexism. Such an anthropology is based on a "truncated human development for both men and women in which both must remain 'half' people who need the other 'half' in order to be 'whole'" (p. 24). The notion of complementarity is based on male-female stereotypes and reflects the "dominance-submission, public-private splits of the patriarchal social order" (p. 24). A philosophy built on complementarity creates a pathological deficiency in males and females so that each is lacking in themselves. It fails to respect the autonomy and individuality of the human person. A philosophy based on equality, however, posits that all sexual love relationships involve two people who are mysteriously and complexly similar as well as different from each other.

The views enunciated by these four Catholic theologians on sexual issues are fairly representative of the position of the progressive or egalitarian school of moral theology in the United States today. They represent a theological challenge that cannot and should not be summarily dismissed by the more moderate or traditional schools because of the growing allegiance to these views among grassroots Catholics.

Analysis

What are the causes of growing attention and interest in the topic of homosexuality in the United States? How can this development be explained? What conditions made it ripe for such changes to occur?

The first factor to be recognized is the influence of grassroots groups of lesbian and gay persons and/or advocacy groups. In each country where the church hierarchy has publicly addressed the issue of homosexuality, these organizations were already in place and served to lobby and influence church leadership. This is a prime example of "theology from below." Such groups were founded in New Zealand, in England (Quest in 1973 and the Catholic Lesbian Sisterhood in 1979), in the Netherlands (the Central Pastoral Working Group in the early 1970s), in Ireland (Reach in 1986), and in the United States (Dignity in 1969, New Ways

Ministry in 1977, Communication Ministry in 1977, the Conference for Catholic Lesbians in 1983, and the Consultation on Homosexuality, Social Justice, and Roman Catholic Theology in 1983). These special interest groups have been larger and earlier in formation in the United States than elsewhere. However, the pastoral ministry provided by organized groups of lesbian and gay Catholics and their advocates is not sufficient in itself to stimulate official structures to respond to the homosexual question. For example, a group called David and Jonathan was founded in France in 1972, Dignité has existed in Canada since the 1970s, and Acceptance was founded in Australia in 1973, yet the national hierarchies of these three countries have not, to date, publicly addressed the homosexual issue.

A second explanation of the importance of the U.S. church in the issue of homosexuality lies in the American culture to which the church must respond in order to shape and mold the values of modern life. The pluralistic culture of the U.S. offers many ways of living and a multitude of social experiences that can result in alternative visions of being church. From its foundation, the United States has valued freedom and reform, has made accommodations for minority groups, and has struggled to adapt existing social structures to meet new needs. Because of the Revolutionary War that broke governmental ties with Great Britain and because of the United States's arrangement of separation of church and state, pluralism is more dominant in the United States than in any other society. This social pluralism has impacted the U.S. church, has resulted in a distinctive religious pluralism, and, in many cases, has caused tensions with a more authoritarian style of leadership. The gay and lesbian liberation movement, which flourished in the United States after 1969, was bound to influence the U.S. church.

A third factor to explain the significance of the U.S. church in the issue of homosexuality, and in many other areas as well, is sheer numbers. The U.S. church possesses more resources, has a larger population and a greater proliferation of ministries to lesbian and gay Catholics than other churches that have begun to deal with this issue.

A fourth element that must be taken into account in this analysis is AIDS. Although AIDS ministry and HIV-AIDS issues are not totally identical to the issue of homosexuality, they are certainly germane because the gay male population in the United States has been severely devastated by this disease. The AIDS epidemic has generated strong calls for compassion and for direct service to AIDS sufferers from more than 10 European hierarchies and other churches in Africa, Asia, Australia, and North America. The Vatican itself sponsored a conference to discuss the epidemic in November 1989. A more complete response to AIDS has moved many individuals and hierarchies to take another related step; i.e., addressing the concerns surrounding homosexuality.

This indirect or backdoor approach to the pastoral and moral development of homosexuality has occurred in the United States and will undoubtedly happen elsewhere. Because of the dramatic numbers of AIDS cases and because the disease was diagnosed earlier among gay males in the United States than in other parts of the world, the U.S. church was moved to a prominent role in the issue of homosexuality. The confluence of the above conditions helps to explain, in part, why the U.S. church has emerged as the leading catalyst in developing issues and questions about the phenomenon of homosexuality in the twentieth century.

Significance
Finally, what significance do these contributions hold for the U.S. church, for the Vatican, and for the Catholic lesbian and gay population?

In the tradition of the melting pot nature and adaptable spirit of American institutions, the U.S. church has demonstrated its ability to adjust again to changing social needs in the present as it did in the past. In the nineteenth century the U.S. church was preoccupied with the education and care of the immigrant population; in the early twentieth century, with the defense of workers' rights. The post-Vatican II church has been faced with a plethora of sexual and gender issues such as contraception, divorce, premarital sex, optional celibacy for priests, priestly ordination of women, and abortion. Homosexuality is one more gender-related issue with which the church must deal.

Wrestling with this complicated social and sexual issue has placed the U.S. church in an uncomfortable middle position. Since the early 1970s American society has become increasingly accepting of homosexuality.

By 1991, 25 states had either decriminalized homosexual behavior conducted in private between consenting adults or had never considered such behavior illegal. In three other states the issue was being litigated in state courts. Scores of cities, counties, and a few states have enacted civil rights legislation to protect lesbian and gay persons in the area of housing, jobs, and public accommodations. Because the Catholic church is the largest U.S. religious institution that condemns homogenital behavior, it has become a symbol of oppression to the lesbian and gay community and a target of public protest by radical groups such as the AIDS Coalition to Unleash Power, popularly called ACT-UP. Because it has tried to foster a more benign interpretation of the homosexual orientation, the U.S. church has been viewed with increasing discomfort by the Vatican. Attempting a delicate balancing act, the U.S. hierarchy is trying to demonstrate to lesbian and gay Catholics a sense of care and compassion while, at the same time, trying to maintain loyalty to Roman expectations. The two goals may be incompatible.

Continuing developments in the U.S. church's approach to homosexuality have undoubtedly had a significant impact on the responses of Roman officials. In December 1975 the Vatican's Congregation for the Doctrine of the Faith found it necessary to address the topic of homosexuality partly in response to the pastoral inroads that Dignity was forging in the United States at that time. Prior to 1975, the Social Action arm of Dignity had approached U.S. bishops and major religious leaders in an attempt to establish a formal dialogue between the institutional church and lesbian and gay Catholics. Again in 1986, the same Congregation saw a need to issue their *Letter to the Bishops of the Catholic Church on the Pastoral Care of Homosexual Persons.* The fact that the letter was written in English, and not in Latin or Italian, led many analysts and commentators to believe that it was directed to the English speaking countries, particularly the United States. They further maintained that it was an attempt to halt the pastoral, theological, and even episcopal developments taking place in the United States (Gramick and Nugent, 1988).

The Vatican seems unable to stem the tide of what it views as the invasion of creeping secular values into the church. On the question of homosexuality, a primary goal is to preserve the traditional condemnation of homogenital acts. The Vatican's employment of its usual means of issuing statements reiterating the tradition seems to have a counterproductive effect in the United States. In 1987, shortly after the Vatican's letter, polls conducted by *Time* magazine and the *Los Angeles Times* indicated that 68% and 67% of Catholics, respectively, agreed with the teaching that homogenital acts are morally wrong. Two years later, after spirited public discussion generated by general nonacceptance of the Vatican letter by the people in the pews and consequent expulsions of Dignity chapters from Catholic church facilities, Catholic support of church teaching banning all homosexual behavior had dropped to only 58%, according to the *San Francisco Examiner*. Some surveys indicate that support is even lower among Catholics under 40 years of age. As in other sexual issues, this reflects a pervasive and serious problem of erosion of Roman authority in the beliefs and practices of U.S. Catholics. This is due largely to an inflexible approach to sexual ethics, based on a very distinct pre-conciliar theology rejected by Vatican II.

Finally, these developments have had a significant effect on lesbian and gay Catholics. The moral judgment on homogenital activity is crucial for most lesbian and gay Catholics. They regard a totally negative evaluation, even within a loving, faithful relationship, as a lack of full equality and basic respect for their personhood. The fact that one U.S. Episcopal document notes that this teaching is not infallible and that the morality of homosexual behavior needs rethinking and development offers some hope to lesbian and gay Catholics that this teaching will one day change (Washington State Catholic Conference, 1983).

The Dutch hierarchy raised a more significant theological challenge to the church's official teaching on homogenital behavior in 1979. At that time, 90% of Dutch Catholics believed that lesbian and gay Catholics in sexual relationships should be considered full members of the church and receive the sacraments. But the contribution of the Dutch church has not dramatically affected the global church because the Dutch Episcopal statement and the views of the people did not receive worldwide circulation. Furthermore, there has been a pronounced and deliberate shift in the composition and approach to ecclesiology of the Dutch hierarchy since 1980. Where there had once been unity between the official and popular church, a rift has gradually developed as the Vatican appointed bishops it considered more orthodox than their predecessors. Of course, in the same period a similar pattern of papal appointees can be detected in the United States. But because the

U.S. episcopal conference is approximately fifty times larger in membership than the Conference of Catholic Bishops of the Netherlands, the pastoral effects of these appointments will take longer to be realized in the United States.

Because of the reaffirmation of the hardened and seemingly inflexible position of the Vatican in 1986 and the eviction of many Dignity chapters from Catholic facilities in the following years, many lesbian and gay Catholics have chosen to leave the church (Gramick, 1988). Their reaction is similar to the response of many of their heterosexual counterparts after the 1968 promulgation by Pope Paul VI of *Humanae Vitae* which reaffirmed the ban against artificial contraception. Others, however, realizing that the U.S. church has made significant pastoral outreach, have decided to remain in the institution, even though they disagree with the teaching that all homogenital activity is intrinsically immoral. After prayerfully examining the truth of their own life experience, they have concluded that their loving sexual relationships not only are compatible with Catholic belief and practice but also provide a source of nourishment for their Christian lives. They are making personal conscience decisions to live out their sexual identity in a healthy, human, and spiritually enriching way. They have come to understand that one can be fully Catholic and still respectfully dissent from non-infallible teaching. Their faith has matured to the point where they are comfortable in making their own decisions and taking responsibility for them. This manner of conflict resolution with church teaching demonstrates that lesbian and gay Catholics have progressed to a stage of moral development in which they accept personal accountability for moral decisions in their lives.

–13–

Old Wine in New Skins?

A recurring criticism of Catholic moral theology in questions of sexuality has been that most of the writing comes from the thinking and experiences of clerical male celibates. Margaret Farley, Lisa Sowle Cahill, Joan Timmerman, Jack Dominian, and James P. Hanigan (1988) are notable exceptions. Hanigan is a married, lay, moral theologian at Duquesne University in Pittsburgh, Pennsylvania.

Hanigan's interest originates from two personal experiences. One was a conversation with a Jesuit priest in gay ministry whom he calls "ethically blind" because the priest, though a compassionate minister, had no "clear idea or conviction about the ethical status of homosexual acts and relationships." The second was a session in his seminar group in which a woman shared her experiences as a lesbian. Both experiences highlighted some of the tensions and conflicts between concrete gay and lesbian individuals and the abstraction of homosexuality, between the demands of traditional Christian morality and practical response in counselling lesbian and gay people.

Hanigan typifies some moral theologians today who are critiquing the traditional teaching on homosexuality and developing new understandings. Because he agrees with the traditional ban on homogenital expression, some argue that the same old wine has been poured into new skins. However, it is important to understand his thinking.

Hanigan sees homosexuality as a "test case" because whatever we say about human sexuality must be tested against the fact of homosexuality and the experiences of gay and lesbian people themselves. For example, if the Good News says that Christian sexuality is joyful hope and loving concern for heterosexual people, it cannot simply say the bad news of "sinner," "tough luck," or "sexual abstinence" to gay and lesbian people. Thus homosexuality, claims Hanigan, "poses today the clearest challenge to the universal and evangelical character" of the Christian sexual ethic. There cannot be one standard for heterosexual people and another for homosexual people. But Hanigan's critique of both magisterial and revisionist thinking does not include acceptance of homosexual acts and relationships. The gospel can be Good News for gay and lesbian people, he believes, "without blessing homosexual acts or transforming a homosexual orientation into a heterosexual one."

Starting with biblical data, Hanigan accepts contemporary scholarship that says there is not clear biblical or rational warrant for assuming that the Hebrew scriptures condemn "all possible homosexual acts and relationships without qualification." Since St. Paul manifests no knowledge of an irreversible homosexual orientation, let alone committed homosexual relationships, it is "simply impossible to know what he would have said about our contemporary questions." He then outlines developments in Catholic teaching on marriage and sexuality, from Pius XI's *Casti Connubii* to Paul VI's *Humanae Vitae*. From his analysis of church teaching on the primary and secondary ends of marriage, he concludes that the good of procreation is related but not absolutely essential to the unitive good. He acknowledges that a biological (sterility) or intentional (rhythm) inability to procreate is no longer a moral barrier to sexual intimacy, since the unitive meaning of sexuality can be realized. At this point, for Hanigan, the developing theological tradition on homosexuality "is open for reevaluation."

Hanigan criticizes magisterial teaching that homosexual acts are "intrinsically disordered and objectively gravely evil" as somewhat arbitrary and authoritarian because it does not face seriously either scriptural problems or the qualifications of teaching on marriage in the last sixty years. Rather the church resorts instead to an appeal to revelation and tradition as "secure sources" of our knowledge about the malice of all homogenital acts. When it acts in this way, Hanigan believes that it loses its right to obedience and credibility.

Hanigan objects to Curran's moderate "compromise" solution and also to the "quality of relationship" approach of many theologians as represented in *A Challenge to Love* (Nugent, 1983). Curran views heterosexuality as "normative," but allows exceptions for "less than ideal" homosexual relationships.

The traditional teaching, based on the Judeo-Christian tradition, holds that human sexuality finds its most complete expression in heterosexuality. Describing heterosexuality as normative means that one ought to strive as much as possible within one's limitations to structure sexuality in that way. Homosexuality, in the most benign judgment, is termed "non-normative." Some who see it as morally justifiable and objectively good in some cases still do not believe that it ought to be afforded the institutional recognition and privileges that heterosexuality enjoys.

The norm arises from a confluence of biblical, theological, psychological, and anthropological sources; others would include historical and experiential sources, as well. An assumption of a heterosexual norm escapes the kind of proof available in the hard sciences. Many proponents of the heterosexual norm are willing to be open to new data, which might make them reconsider the norm. It is important to recall that at one time, and even today in some quarters, maleness and whiteness were held to be the norm for authentic humanity and full personhood. The same sources used to defend heterosexuality as the norm were once employed to defend the other norms.

Traditional theologians like Hanigan will acknowledge a gradual and organic development in magisterial teaching on human sexuality. They are unwilling, however, to view as "organic" a development that would affirm homosexuality on an equal basis with heterosexuality in every way or as a part of God's plan for humanity. For them this would entail a radical and unjustified redefinition and understanding of the human person and human sexual differentiation.

In this way the traditionalists differ from most of the theological contributors to *A Challenge to Love*. These contributors argue for a normative status for homosexual relationships equal to heterosexual ones. They hold that meaning and value for all sexual interactions come not from sexual forms, but from the concrete impact on human persons. In such a view, the biological, sexual differentiation is simply not an essential component in ethical-moral evaluation.

Hanigan argues that there is no positive right to sexual satisfaction, fulfillment, or happiness, but only the right to pursue these

goods unobstructed and within reason. Thus, the means employed
in their pursuit cannot be justified simply because they are the only
means by which these goods can be realized, as Curran has argued.
Curran seems to assume the moral goodness, or indifference, of
homosexual acts as a means to an objective good, rather than
proving the goodness of the means first. For Hanigan, if homosexual acts/unions are to be justified, they should have the same moral status as heterosexual unions and on the same basic grounds.

Hanigan acknowledges that the "quality of relationship"
school rightly emphasizes the interpersonal quality of the sexual
relationship as a key moral consideration; but he argues that this
approach neglects the specific sexual character of the acts and relationships it evaluates, and ignores or denies the "revelatory
character of our human sexual natures." This is where he begins
to reveal his own stance and to lay the groundwork for his ultimately negative, though finely tuned, judgment. His position is
based on the physical (structural and systemic receptivity of the
vagina) and biological (mutual contributions to procreation) complementarity of male and female sexuality which, for him, has primary and normative moral significance.

Hanigan situates his own approach to homosexuality in a discussion of sexuality as vocation. Sexual behavior is related to a
"way of life" as married, single heterosexual, or consecrated celibate, and that way of life is a specification of our vocation to love
and service. The traditional ideal for human sexual activity in its
most complete, self-giving expression in sexual intercourse is that
it be "the ritual sign of a publicly acknowledged, mutually committed and fully shared life." Sexual intercourse embodies, sym-
bolizes, and celebrates all this even apart from children. Marriage,
not the birth of children, is the sign of Christ's union with the
church. The fundamental question for Hanigan is this: can homosexual expressions and unions bring about this two-in-one flesh

and be symbolic realization of a vocation? The heart of his argument is found in the chapters "Vocation and Homosexual Relationships" and "Ritual Authenticity." If homosexual expressions can be understood as a "graced calling oriented to the service of God's people," then they can enjoy normative status for sexually active people; if not, they must be judged incompatible with a Christian way of life.

Before arguing this latter position, Hanigan offers some disclaimers. He does not deny that there are humanly tender, caring, loving, and dedicated homosexual relationships, nor does he question that such people can be outgoing in their care for and service to others. Although he does not doubt the actual existence and testimonies of such couples, he insists that such admissions cannot settle theological issues. It is not a question of gay and lesbian couples not being sexually faithful and exclusive, accepting sex as a gift, or accepting social responsibility for any consequences of their sexual activity. The crux of the issue for Hanigan is the claim that homosexual activity must be an essential aspect of their vocational calling with both social and personal import. He does not believe that sexual expression is essential in homosexual relationships; if present, then its import can be only personal and private, not social as in marriage.

Hanigan argues that there can be no "two-in-one flesh unity" in homosexual relationships: not ritually in the sexual act, not substantially in the unity and shared differences of male and female, and not in the new life of a child. Since the first is his strongest argument, I will comment on them in reverse order.

He has already admitted that the inability to procreate is not of "definitive significance" in ruling out all homosexual acts. Yet for some unexplained reason, he is still not ready to concede that a true homosexual orientation is a "good reason" to "override the deliberate refusal of openness to the possibility that is manifested by one's choosing to act sexually in certain ways." Why does Hanigan draw the line at same-sex couples and not at sterile couples? Is the "deliberate refusal of openness" to procreation more blameworthy or less justifiable because it originates in a psychological state of homosexual identity rather than in a physiological state of sterility? Does he believe that sterile heterosexual acts are somehow "open" to new life? Is the fact that lesbian and gay people choose not to procreate by reason of their erotic and emotional attractions not to be accounted as responsible and praiseworthy? It would seem that this objection depends on his basic premise that the only physical form of sexual expression that can be morally good is penis-vagina, regardless of procreation.

Hanigan's second claim is that a homosexual relationship cannot substantially be a "two-in-one flesh unity." The same-sex couple's oneness is that of friendship. Friendship does not require or depend on sexual acts. Sexual activity is "not essential" and "often a distraction." He is most vulnerable here to a charge of either theorizing from insufficient experience or of ignoring or negating the testimony of gay and lesbian couples. His argument is that, if sex is essential to the friendship, then the "unconditional nature" of the friendship is called into question. He recognizes the presence of both friendship and sex in heterosexual marriage, but he is unwilling to perceive a similar experience in a same-sex relationship. He insists that the difference and unity of homosexual friendship is not "sexual," but what he really means is that it is not *genital*. But is that the controlling and decisive difference? According to the Jungians, for instance, each of us has both male and female qualities and even physical vestiges of the other sex. Is it not possible that some other kinds of complementarity or unity and difference exist in a same-sex couple based not on their genitals, but on their male and female personae?

Hanigan's third and final claim about "ritual authenticity" is the key to his entire case, which rests on the importance we attach to the physical differences in the male-female sexual differentiation. He believes that same-sex couples can only simulate or imitate the authentic penis-vagina ritual of sexual love. Hanigan cites André Guindon (1977) who compared sexuality to speech and language and suggested that homosexual interactions are a form of stuttering. He seems unaware that Guindon (1986) has moved away from earlier judgments about homosexuality and now talks of fecundity as the principal component of all healthy human sexuality, including homosexuality. More recently, Guindon (1988) has gone further still and chosen to criticize the use of "homosexual acts" as physical behavior or material performances that have an evil meaning independent of any user's meaning-making operation. For Guindon, it is better to speak of "gay speech" in which behavior is a kind of communication. For a gay person, then, self-expression and communication are "homosexual acts." Gay and lesbian people cannot simply remain silent. But what forms of their speech are permissible and which forbidden? The criterion of physical acts is an inadequate understanding of sexual expression and communication between human beings.

For Hanigan, the ritual act of sexual intercourse and the "materials" of penis and vagina for the ritual must have the capacity to symbolize the reality they would make present. It is there that the complementarity of human sexuality (read: physical parts) becomes crucial. In Hanigan's thinking, heterosexual complementarity remains the Christian tradition's primary metaphor for understanding human love and sexuality. His case rests on the assumption that the only fully human and moral form of sexual behavior is penis-vagina intercourse. If we cast his argument in terms of "language," it would echo the approach of John Paul II who speaks of the nuptial meaning or language of the human body in explaining Catholic teaching on sexuality.

Some are suggesting the metaphor be opened up with new understandings of human sexuality that transcend the biological and physical differences as not essential to sexual union and ethical evaluations. Cannot homosexual unions also be complementary in certain ways such as mutual self-giving? Cannot complementarity have a wider meaning than just biological? To deny this *a priori* is to ignore the intrinsic experience of countless gay and lesbian Christians.

Monika Hellwig (1987) has termed the traditional metaphor for understanding sexuality the "anatomical toy-maker myth." She describes it thus: "God has created people according to a blueprint which is written in their bodies, in their anatomy; they are made to operate in a certain way and, when they operate in that way, their mission and purpose is fulfilled; they return to the hands of their Creator in peace and God is glorified" (pp. 12-13).

But another myth has come upon the scene: "God creates human persons in the divine image by awakening them into freedom, self-determination and creativity, in which they discover that they are essentially relational and that their humanity is realized in the ways they shape the earth, themselves, one another, and their societies; in this they are fulfilling and realizing the creativity of God; when they shape communities which offer liberation, happiness and fulfilling relationships to all, they fulfill the purpose of creation; then all creation is drawn into a great harmony and returns to the Creator in peace, and God is glorified" (Hellwig, 1987, p. 13).

Determining whether the new myth accords with the gospel and tradition is a task for theologians working collaboratively with the magisterium. It is not a question to be settled by ecclesiastical authorities in isolation from theologians. The criteria for evaluating the new myth must come from the gospel, the church's tradition, and the consciousness of believers. Relationality, not anatomy, is the basis of the new myth or metaphor. This relationality is rooted in the relationship of the Trinity and was described more fully in Chapter 11.

Despite Hanigan's ultimate rejection of homosexual acts and relationships on official levels, he makes some assertions that seem to seriously undermine his previous arguments. He says, for example, that he does not know how to determine beyond question whether homosexuality is, psychologically viewed, a pathology or a "natural and normal sexual difference." If homosexuality is natural, then he would be forced to accept that the genital acts of same-sex couples are also ritually authentic.

Hanigan believes that homosexual activity is not intrinsic to a call to love one another, and wonders what homosexual couples are "re-creating, enhancing and celebrating" by their sexual acts. In another place, he acknowledges that while most people experience a desire for intimacy and oneness with persons of the opposite sex, lesbian and gay people experience the same towards others of the same sex. Yet he does not draw the logical conclusion that same-sex couples might be re-creating, enhancing and celebrating exactly what heterosexual couples do: their desire for intimacy and oneness.

Hanigan disagrees with the 1986 Vatican letter on homosexuality that calls the inclinations "objectively disordered" because he does not believe homosexual desires are ontically flawed. Since he cannot affirm with certitude that a homosexual orientation is a "physical, psychological, moral or spiritual aberration," he cannot conclude that the orientation is an ontic evil. Ontic evil is a lack of a good that is due as essential to my well being. Because biological children are not essential to everyone's well being, according to Hanigan, the lack of procreative possibilities in homosexual relationships does not constitute ontic evil. What Hanigan does term ontic evil in a homosexual relationship is the absence of

vocational integrity. He describes this as a graced calling oriented
to the service of God's people. But his argument here depends on
his *a priori* exclusion of homosexual acts and relationships from
the ability to be interpersonal and to serve God and neighbor.

In three concluding chapters Hanigan nuances his earlier judgments about homosexual acts and relationships. He says it is impossible to declare all homosexual acts and relationships "gravely
sinful of their very nature." Although no public recognition can
be accorded them at present because they lack objectively full vocational integrity, they do have personal and moral, rather than
social, significance. Evaluating their sinfulness is "a matter for the
judgment of personal conscience informed by the teaching of the
Church." These relationships may be, in the lives of particular gay
and lesbian couples, "a sign and a service of one's Christian disci-
pleship" and "steps toward the ideal and toward a fuller understanding and acceptance of one's sexuality as part of one's
Christian vocation." In the end, that comes rather close to
acknowledging that homosexual relationships can embody full
vocational integrity.

Hanigan's views are worth reading and re-reading. The fact
that his book makes a small volume does not mean that its appeal
is at the merely popular level. Its major contribution to professional theological discussion is in the way it frames the central argument of physical and biological complementarity that the
magisterium has recently emphasized in defending traditional
teachings in a personalistic approach. The chief weakness of Hanigan's work is to leave one with an impression of inner contradic-
tions and tensions between various assertions. This may stem
from the tension between a real empathy for the situation of
homosexual persons and a commitment to, if not some bias for,
the traditional understanding of human sexuality.

Hanigan admits that his argument is not put forward "as conclusive beyond all question or doubt." There are "many points," he says, "that are not sufficiently developed, many claims that require further substantiation." He concludes with a frank admission that there might be exceptions to the normative ideal of heterosexuality which did not contravene the will of God. It may be that homosexual relationships do have a vocational significance that has been overlooked or misunderstood. Gay and lesbian Christians and others are asking the church to consider this possibility. Hanigan sees arguments that would place homosexuality on an equal footing with heterosexuality as standing apart from biblical and theological tradition. They would, for him, seem to entail a culturally dominant understanding of human life and destiny. At the same time he urges pastoral dialogue and continued theological discussion that are open to the reactions and proposals of all the faithful. His book is a serious and important study; it demands both attention and a serious response.

–14–

Lesbian/Gay Theology and Spirituality: The New Frontier

Although a gay and lesbian spirituality began to be formally constructed only since the late 1970s, lesbian and gay persons long incarnated a spirituality that put them uniquely in touch with the transcendent. Carlo Coccioli's (1966) novel, *Fabrizio Lupo*, which appeared in many European countries in the 1950s and 1960s, describes in poetic images the nobility of a gay man confident of his love relationship with his God but struggling to feel reconciled with his Catholic church. The religious ideals of individuals like Fabrizio Lupo were once shrouded in the shadows of the early and late Middle Ages but have recently been documented historically (Boswell, 1980). With the advent of a bold, new, theological enterprise, the lesbian and gay spiritual treasury has begun to be explored and systematically recorded.

In the 1960s, classical European and North American Catholic theologians were confronted with a novel kind of theology from Latin America. This liberation theology, as it was called, gave rise to a wide variety of social justice groups and human rights causes. Its architects began with the lived experience of the Third World's poor, oppressed, and marginalized, instead of with the position of the powerful and the privileged. As theologians like Gustavo Gutierrez, the Boff brothers, and Jon Sobrino articulated the needs of the economically and politically exploited, the church was able to get a "view from below."

Besides the materially poor, other groups that felt outside the mainstream of social and ecclesiastical power soon began to forge theologies and spiritualities based on their own understandings of reality. Women and African Americans, in particular, questioned the traditional assumptions on which church teachings were built. Today, courses on feminist and black theologies and spiritualities are finding their way into the curriculums of many divinity schools and major universities.

The Starting Point

In its development over centuries of Christian life and thought, classical European theology relied predominantly on such notions as nature, reason, and authority. Unlike traditional theology, which is essentially a deductive science, liberation theology takes an inductive or "theology from below" approach. Each of these two kinds of theology utilizes and integrates different fields of knowledge into its corpus. In classical theology, Thomas Aquinas virtually baptized the philosophy of Aristotle; other doctors of the church and the early Church Fathers borrowed heavily from Greek,

Roman, or Near-Eastern thought. Liberation theology draws not only from the ancient philosophers but also from modern political science, particularly the economic analysis of Karl Marx. Feminist and black theologies add the tools of various psychologies and anthropologies.

Likewise, we would naturally expect that lesbian and gay people, another socially stigmatized group, would begin to evolve a theology and a spirituality from their own particular experience. Sexual orientation is not an exhaustive component of one's personality. But it is a significant element that colors an individual's approach and response to the world and his or her understanding of God, community, and society. One's sexual orientation also affects others' responses to the individual. As such, sexual orientation is a critical element that must be taken into account in one's spiritual life and in the theological life of the Christian community.

Historically, gay and lesbian people have not been recognized as a category of person. Boswell (1989) distinguishes three categories of persons who diverge from the accepted norm: distinguishable insiders, inferior insiders, and outsiders. Distinguishable insiders are those who are different from the majority because of a particular trait but suffer no disadvantage because of it. Eye or hair color is an obvious example. Redheads or blue-eyed persons are distinguishable, but society does not legally discriminate against anyone who possesses either of these features.

The second category, inferior insiders, includes those persons who are recognized within the social establishment but are definitely treated in a socially inferior manner because they deviate from the norm designated by the ruling class. In a dominant white male society, women and people of racial or ethnic minorities are examples of inferior insiders.

Outsiders, the third category of persons, are despised by the ruling majority. Their existence is either unacknowledged or not tolerated. Jewish people in Nazi Germany and lesbian and gay people in most of the world today are examples of such outsiders.

Until the end of the nineteenth century there was no category to conceptualize lesbian and gay persons because most of humankind believed that all people were basically heterosexually oriented. Without a recognized category to name them as distinct, lesbian and gay people were hampered in their ability to transmit a historical legacy to future generations. As long as there was no category to name lesbian and gay individuals, they were prevented from sharing their stories and thus from developing a distinctive spirituality.

Only with Sigmund Freud did the professional world acknowledge the existence of a lesbian or gay personality, and then only as a deviation from the established norm of heterosexuality. A century later, the designation of deviancy has all but disappeared in professional spheres in North America and parts of Europe. However, homosexuality is still considered deviant behavior on the popular level. It is precisely at the grassroots level where lesbian and gay persons usually encounter prejudice and discrimination when their sexual orientation is known or suspected. Society relegates them to the category of outsiders, but at least lesbian and gay people now form a category and can move to develop their own spirituality and theology.

How can the Christian churches justify any theology that ignores the experience of more than one hundred million lesbian and gay Christians? How can we be complacent with church structures that accept heterosexual persons but punish lesbian and gay persons when they are true to their natures? How can we claim that the Christian churches are following the gospel of Jesus if Christianity aggravates the alienation from the faith community that lesbian and gay persons face? Should not Christians welcome lesbian and gay people in the name of Jesus?

A Lesbian/Gay Theology and Spirituality

Christian theology has traditionally begun by positing an ideal, objective, and absolute world of reality against which the morality of individual human acts is measured. Liberation theology stretches our moral horizon by naming sinful structures in which individuals are often trapped, and by working for their transformation. This often results in social and ecclesial conflict.

A lesbian/gay theology or spirituality begins, I believe, with a sociological analysis taken from the theory of symbolic interactionism (Plummer, 1975). This theory includes the following three major tenets: Human beings act on the basis of meanings. Meanings flow from social interaction with other human beings. Meanings are continuously changed through a process of interpretation.

In this theory "meanings," although of central importance, are constantly in flux, subjective, and relative. Any lesbian/gay theology or spirituality then, which begins from the experience of lesbian and gay persons, must ask the question, "What does it *mean* to be lesbian or gay?" The dominant culture, which has categorized the lesbian and gay person as an outsider, has defined homosexuality in negative terms. The meanings traditionally assigned to homosexuality have varied from sickness and abnormality to sinfulness and crime.

But the lesbian/gay experience questions and challenges these negative meanings of homosexuality. How do we arrive at a definition of what is normal and what is deviant? What are the criteria of health and what is illness? Who legislates what actions are considered criminal offenses against the state and how do we determine what constitutes evil or sin? Obviously, the ruling class has a vested interest in asserting that all those who do not meet their requirements of acceptability are labeled deviant. In effect, any dominant group, whether civil or ecclesiastical, can create deviants by making certain rules, with or without justification.

The violator of these rules is labeled an outsider and a deviant. The sociologists Gagnon and Simon (1968) observed, "There is no form of sexual activity that is not deviant at some time, in some social location, in some specified relationships, or with some partners" (p. 107).

A positive and affirming lesbian/gay theology or spirituality rejects the notion that a homosexual orientation is abnormal, sick, sinful, or criminal. The 1986 letter from the Vatican's Congregation for the Doctrine of the Faith, which contended that a homosexual orientation was "objectively disordered," obviously did not begin from the experience of being lesbian or gay. Such experience confirms that a homosexual orientation is not contrary to nature but is part of God's plan for creation and essential for developing the human family. Without the presence of lesbian and gay people in the world, reality would be truncated and humankind unfulfilled. These assertions are based on the testimony of lesbian and gay Christians and the witness of their lives (Curb & Manahan, 1985; Gramick, 1983, 1989; McNaught, 1988; McNeill, 1988; Zanotti, 1986).

The development of an adequate lesbian/gay theology and spirituality will contribute significantly to the Christian community. A number of writers have begun to explore this new frontier (Fortunato, 1982; Glaser, 1990; Heyward, 1982, 1987, 1989; McNeill, 1988; Woods, 1977). The ravages that AIDS has visited on the gay male community can be, and have been, transformed into opportunities for joining with Christ in his own pilgrimage of suffering and death (Nugent, 1989). Lesbian/feminist theologians are exposing the limitations of a procreative sexual ethic and are suggesting instead an ethic based on mutual relation. Same-sex couples have a greater potential for modeling this ethic than opposite sex couples who are often subtly saddled with societal conditioning to conform to sex-role stereotypes involving dominance and submission. A lesbian/gay theology, moreover, challenges the church to be truly catholic and to embrace all people, including sexual and racial minorities. In a truly Catholic community, there are no outsiders or inferior insiders. There are only insiders who are distinguishable for the various gifts they bring to the Body of Christ.

Spirituality is like the oil of gladness or the springs of living water that well up from a person's faith experience with God and the world. It is no accident that the scriptures use these earthly metaphors to express a reality that is found by reaching deep into one's own soul. A lesbian/gay spirituality or theology begins with the individual's encounter with God. It is not necessary that God's presence be mediated through formal religious structures. Although God frequently uses religious institutions to communicate with people, such avenues are often blocked in the case of lesbian and gay persons when these institutions choose to make lesbian and gay people outsiders. These outsiders often learn to seek God without a mediator by developing a deep, personal relationship with God.

Scripture

A scriptural hermeneutics of suspicion recognizes that what we see depends upon where we are standing. A lesbian/gay theology is an example of authentic subversion. It involves a real turning from below with a scriptural analysis from the underside of society. Since God's spirit is continually revealing truth to the human heart, the scriptures contain some insights that can be made known to the Christian community only through the testimony of lesbian and gay people.

In their personal encounter with the living God, lesbian and gay people must read the scriptures in a new way. They have a need to study, to pray, and to interpret the scriptures in the light of their own experience. The Exodus story and Jesus' announcement of his mission describe a God who definitely sides with the oppressed. In a lesbian/gay interpretation of the story of the Israelites' bondage in Egypt, the servants in Pharaoh's court become individuals, afraid of sexuality and homosexuality, who try to reinforce guilt and shame on lesbian and gay people.

Jesus' sermon in the synagogue at Nazareth proclaimed release for the captives and liberty for the downtrodden. These words should bring comfort and hope to those held captive by self-hatred or low self-esteem. Jesus comes to offer new life and a positive sense of identity to those who are sexually different. When Jesus read from the prophet Isaiah and added that those scriptures came true that day in him, the Jews were furious and ejected him from the synagogue (Luke 4:16-30). In his ministry of teaching and healing, Jesus challenged the authority of the religious leaders of his day. By the witness of their lives of faith, responsibility, and love, lesbian and gay Christians similarly reject traditional teachings regarding the moral status of homogenital acts and thus threaten the authority of contemporary religious structures. Like Jesus, many Dignity members were expelled from Catholic church property after the organization declared at a 1987 national convention that lesbian and gay people may express their sexuality "physically in a unitive manner that is loving, life-giving and life-affirming."

When Jesus' adversaries tried to trick him by asking who is one's neighbor, Jesus told the parable of the good Samaritan who cared for the man attacked and beaten by robbers (Luke 10:25-37). The Samaritan, despised and shunned by self-respecting Jews, has a modern analogue in lesbian and gay people who are found in greater than expected proportions in healing and service-related professions. Perhaps drag queens, effeminate gay males, and butchy dykes, the most scorned of lesbian and gay persons, have most to teach the Christian community about the meaning of being a neighbor. We see this in the character of the female impersonator, Alban, in the Broadway play *La Cage aux Folles*. Ridiculed by society, Alban shows kindness, understanding, and acceptance of the human condition to the other characters in the play.

The Hebrew scriptures also reveal new truths when examined in a lesbian/gay context. The book of Esther tells of a beautiful Jewish queen who is a symbol of hope and salvation for her people. The Gentile king's prime minister hates the Jews and arranges for the king to sign a decree ordering all Jews to be slain. Esther cleverly appeals to the king, gets him to reverse his decree, and saves her people from execution. The king could easily represent some members of the church hierarchy who are often kind but misguided men. Esther may portend lesbian and gay Christians who, through their perseverance and devotion to humanity, may eventually prevail upon church leaders to change their current approach to sexuality and sexual ethics that is placing unnecessary and unrealistic burdens on God's people. Just as Esther saved her people, lesbian and gay Christians will save the church by enabling the faith community to make peace with their sexuality and to cease an emotional destruction of human lives. There will be a lessening of anxiety, denial, and repression of sexual feelings in favor of a more human and personalist appreciation of the meaning of sexuality. The entire faith community will grow into a freedom that relates sexuality not to duty, procreation, violence, or guilt, but to love.

We read in the Hebrew scriptures that the Israelites often fell into the practice of idolatry. They bowed before a golden calf and called it a god. Some people today have fashioned a god from their own obsessions, one of which is an absolute and rigid approach to sexuality. Lesbian and gay persons remind the Christian community that God alone is absolute. Those who cling

to an inflexible heterosexism, who fear a world in which heterosexuality is not thought to be a superior form of sexuality, fail to
reverence other human beings properly. Heterosexuality is their
god.

Theological and Spiritual Frontiers

Lesbian and gay Christians must begin to articulate an alternative
spiritual and theological vision that will be taken seriously by the
larger Christian community. To effect this transformation, lesbian
and gay Christians need a supportive atmosphere and a
community to encourage, nourish, and reflect upon personal
communications with God. Many Dignity chapters, which have
spirituality committees, provide a loving space to integrate the
spiritual and sexual lives of their members. After centuries of
oppression, it is necessary to heal their wounds and to celebrate
the unique gift of God they are.

Although decades, perhaps centuries, may be needed for the
accomplishment of such a task, there is cause for optimism and
hope. Within the last twenty years in Western society, lesbian and
gay people have left the shadows of invisibility for the public
sphere. Lesbian and gay literature, art, and culture is being re-
claimed. Lesbian and gay social, political, and religious groups
have been formed. Domestic partner relationships, with the legal
rights and benefits accruing to same-sex couples, have been acknowledged by several large cities in the United States. These social developments portend a future conducive to spiritual and
theological change. Only when lesbian and gay persons have been
accorded full and equal respect and dignity as human beings in
society and in the church so that they are no longer categorized as
inferior insiders or outsiders, will the Christian community be
able to say that the god of heterosexism has been eradicated. Only
when there is no societal, economic, or religious prejudice felt by

an individual because of his or her sexual orientation, gender, color, religious, or political beliefs, can the church claim that humankind is beginning to feel on this earth the freedom of the daughters and sons of God.

Postscript

Since 1971 we have been engaged in both part-time and full-time ministry with gay and lesbian Catholics and with the plethora of institutions and personalities that comprise the unique and rich expression of Catholicism in the United States. From the very beginning we have repeatedly been asked two questions: How did you get involved in this ministry? Why do you continue? The answers are rather simple. We both believe the Lord called us in different ways to engage in a public ministry with and on behalf of a group of people who have traditionally been neglected or abused by some segments of the church. Despite occasional setbacks or some active opposition, we continue because we have seen gradual and positive developments in attitudes and practices in the church. We realized long ago that we were in it for the long haul. Whatever contributions we might make will probably not realize their cumulative effect until long after we are gone from the scene. One plants; one waters; another reaps.

In 1971 Jeannine met a young, gay, Catholic man in Philadelphia named Dominic Bash who had spent some time in a religious community. He asked her point blank, "What is the Catholic church doing for my gay brothers and sisters?" That question and challenge led her to read, study, and participate in meetings on the topic of homosexuality. Eventually it led to meetings with a group of Roman Catholic and Anglican gay men while she pursued doctoral studies in mathematics education at the University of Pennsylvania. Depending on which of us is relating the origin myth of our initiation into gay and lesbian ministry, we call it either "The Dominic Story" or the "Adam and Eve Story."

A newspaper account of Jeannine's work appeared in the *Philadelphia Bulletin* in the fall of 1971. She received more than a dozen supportive responses. One came from Bob Nugent, a Philadelphia diocesan priest who was in transition from parish work to an unofficial leave of absence to explore non-parochial ministerial possibilities. Bob was living with the De LaSalle Christian Brothers in Elkins Park, Pennsylvania, as their chaplain. He was pursuing graduate studies at Temple and Villanova Universities and doing volunteer work at a skid row hospice. In his letter of encouragement to Jeannine, Bob obliquely, and not really all too seriously, offered to help out. Two days later Jeannine called and asked Bob to come to the meetings. Hence, the "Adam and Eve Story." Bob began to meet with some of the individuals in the group for counseling, confessions, and home liturgies. Revs. Paul Morrissey, O.S.A., Myron Judy, O. Carm., and John Cimino, O. Praem., were also working pastorally with the group. Eventually the Philadelphia chapter of Dignity emerged when the Anglo-Roman Catholic group split into two distinct organizations.

In 1972 Jeannine returned to Baltimore to begin a teaching career in mathematics at the College of Notre Dame of Maryland administered by the School Sisters of Notre Dame. In the fall of that year she was instrumental in initiating a chapter of Dignity in Washington, D.C. The following year, along with Joseph Hughes, a Baltimore diocesan priest, she co-founded the Baltimore chapter of Dignity. The first Mass for the Baltimore chapter was celebrated in the chapel of St. Jerome's Convent where Jeannine lived with four other School Sisters of Notre Dame who supported her ministry. The chapter continued to meet at the convent until they were eventually welcomed in Baltimore diocesan parishes.

Meanwhile both of us continued to read and learn about homosexuality and began to write and lecture on issues of pastoral care for gay and lesbian persons. We lobbied actively for the passage of bills to protect their civil rights. Jeannine testified in support of a gay rights bill in Baltimore, which caused Archbishop William Borders, who publicly opposed the bill, to register a complaint with Jeannine's provincial administrator. Bob was the first priest in the Archdiocese of Philadelphia to testify in support of a gay civil rights bill at the City Council hearings. His action did not please Cardinal John Krol, who sent the priest-director of the Archdiocesan Family Life Bureau to testify against the bill. After continued pressure from the archdiocese Bob joined the Society of the Divine Savior in 1975 and moved to Washington, D.C., to participate in a formation program. He was given faculties from the archdiocese for pastoral work. While in Washington he worked with the local Dignity chapter in liturgy and counseling and was instrumental in negotiating for Dignity to worship on the campus of Georgetown University. At the same time he was on the staff of the Quixote Center, a newly founded peace and justice center whose co-director was Rev. William Callahan.

In 1976, Jeannine, feeling a call to move from the academic to the social justice arena, joined the Quixote Center staff. The other staff members encouraged us to collaborate on gay-lesbian projects under the auspices of the Quixote Center. Our main work during this period was a basic workshop on homosexuality designed primarily for people in pastoral ministry in the Washington-

Baltimore area. We called the programs "New Ways Workshops." We took the name from a 1976 pastoral letter on sexuality from Brooklyn's Bishop Francis Mugavero who urged the church to find "new ways to communicate the truth of Christ" to people dealing with homosexuality and other sexual issues.

As the requests for talks, programs, and retreats began to escalate, we decided to devote all our time and resources to this underdeveloped area of church life because there was no other Catholic justice group working fulltime on this issue. So in the summer of 1977 a not-for-profit educational organization was formed, appropriately baptized New Ways Ministry, and incorporated in the state of Maryland in May 1978. Initially we volunteered our time at New Ways Ministry while working in other ministries to support ourselves financially. In the fall of 1977 Jeannine taught mathematics at the University of Maryland. From 1977-1979, Bob worked in campus ministry at the College of Notre Dame of Maryland and returned to D.C. periodically to work at New Ways Ministry.

In 1978, Bob was informed by the Archdiocese of Washington that his faculties were being withdrawn because he no longer resided there. Despite repeated requests for faculties for preaching and hearing clergy confessions, they were not granted. The chancery finally acknowledged that the real reason for the denial of faculties was his continued association with New Ways Ministry.

In 1978, Jeannine secured a $38,000 grant from the National Institute of Mental Health for a study of the coming out process and coping strategies of lesbian women. This not only helped put the fledgling organization on a sound financial basis, but also drew the first public criticism from church authorities in Washington, D.C. The editor of the diocesan paper, basing his opposition on an inaccurate story about the grant in the *Washington Star*, wrote that he found the study "distressing" because it assumed that "being a practicing homosexual is a valid expression of a person's lifestyle." The *Star* had interpolated the word "practicing," which appeared nowhere in the New Ways Ministry press release. The diocesan paper did eventually publish a letter of clarification from us. This was to be the first of a long series of continuing problems with the Archdiocese of Washington. One of the first national projects we developed was a Catholic response to the 1978 Anita Bryant anti-gay campaign in Dade County, Florida. It involved public support of a statement for civil rights and pastoral care that was endorsed by more than three thousand Catholic groups and individuals. The project was called a Catholic Coalition for Gay Civil Rights. Around the same time we produced the first of our many collaborative publishing efforts in *A Time to Speak,* a small collection of positive statements from Catholic organizations and prominent individuals in the church supporting ministry and civil rights for lesbian and gay people.

In the spring of 1979, at the request of a Catholic sister working in a retreat house ministry, New Ways Ministry sponsored a private weekend retreat for gay women religious. After discreet initial publicity, the Chancellor of the Archdiocese of Washington sent a memo to all the bishops and to the major superiors of men's and women's communities about the ecclesiastical status of New Ways Ministry and "the Don Quixote Center." Without mentioning the retreat, the memo said that the two organizations were not approved. We soon began to realize that we were not going to be very popular in the Archdiocese of Washington! In April, New Ways Ministry released its own memo to all U. S. bishops and religious superiors which outlined its history, goals, and projects. In the meantime, the Vatican intervened and instructed our major superiors in Rome to order us to cancel the retreat. The retreat, however, was held as planned.

In 1980 we began our ventures into international collaboration
on the topic. After a 1979 fact-finding visit to England and the
Netherlands where we met Bishop Augustine Harris and Catholic
laity and clergy involved in ministry with gay and lesbian Catholics, we published *Homosexual People in Society*, a discussion document from a committee of the Dutch bishops, and later *An Introduction to the Pastoral Care of Homosexual Persons* from the bishops
of England and Wales. This last document has had a strong influence on statements from several U. S. dioceses.

Following a New Ways Ministry critique of a letter on vocations by the bishops of New England, we received our first letter
of episcopal support.

In 1981, in cooperation with Dignity, we published what we
humorously call the gay catechism, *Homosexual Catholics: A Primer
for Discussion*. This highly popular booklet was written in cooperation with the late Thomas Oddo, C.S.C., past president of the
University of Portland and former secretary of the national Dignity
organization, who was tragically killed in an auto collision in 1989.

In 1980, Bishop James Hickey from Cleveland was appointed
Archbishop of Washington when Cardinal William Baum was
assigned to a Vatican post. In June and again in September of that
year, we wrote to request a meeting with the Archbishop to familiarize him with our work. A meeting was promised but never
materialized until publicity went out for the First National Symposium on Homosexuality and the Catholic Church. Scheduled
for November 9-11, 1981, this first national event of its kind was
co-sponsored by approximately 50 religious congregations and
national Catholic organizations. In September, we received a call
from the archbishop's secretary to inform us that we had an
appointment with the Archbishop in two days at his private residence. The only meeting we both had with Archbishop Hickey
took place on September 30, 1981. We assumed it was to be a pri-

vate dialogue and came alone. The archbishop arrived with his chancellor, Msgr. John Donohue, and John R. Connery, S.J., a moral theologian. We discussed the archbishop's agenda but not the topics we asked to be placed on the agenda. At the time we were not politically seasoned enough to realize that the procedure put us at a disadvantage from the outset. We agreed to provide the archbishop with more information on our programs and expressed the hope that this meeting would be the first in an ongoing dialogue.

Within a month Archbishop Hickey informed all the U.S. bishops and religious congregations that New Ways Ministry was "ambiguous" on the issue of homosexuality (meaning homogenital acts) and discouraged attendance at the symposium. He suggested that religious communities withdraw their endorsements, but not one did.

The symposium was originally scheduled to be held at Holy Trinity Mission Seminary in Silver Spring, Maryland. Early registration indicated that we would outgrow that facility. Approximately three weeks before the event, and without knowledge of the archbishop's efforts to influence the Trinitarian provincial to prohibit our use of the Seminary, we decided to move the meeting to the National 4-H Center in Bethesda, Maryland. After initially agreeing, senior officials at the 4-H Center refused to host the event. New Ways Ministry subsequently sued the National 4-H Center in the U. S. District Court but lost. In the course of the litigation, Ron Bogard, legal counsel for New Ways Ministry, uncovered evidence that the Washington Archdiocese communicated to the 4-H Center that New Ways Ministry was "not approved."

Fortunately we were able to secure a downtown hotel approximately a week before the scheduled date. The First National Symposium on Homosexuality and the Catholic Church was held on Nov. 9-11, 1981, with approximately 200 participants and coverage by the Catholic and secular press. In 1983, we prepared for a second symposium. Two bishops agreed to speak at the event provided that Archbishop Hickey would at least remain neutral. One bishop advised Jeannine to meet with the archbishop to propose the idea and ascertain his reaction. The meeting took place, but the archbishop was distressed that Jeannine was accompanied by Blythe Batten and Thomas Hlas, staff members from New Ways Ministry. He would meet only with her. The question of the two bishops' participation in a second symposium was never broached because the archbishop spent most of the time explaining why he believed Jeannine should leave lesbian/gay ministry.

Archbishop Hickey then requested our congregational leadership at the provincial and general levels to remove us from the Washington Archdiocese and from lesbian/gay ministry. Throughout this time he was in communication with two Roman congregations about our work. Bob took a sabbatical in 1982-83 and Jeannine in 1983-84 as cooling off periods while we tried to negotiate a resolution satisfactory to all. At the request of the Superior General of the School Sisters of Notre Dame, the archbishop's theologian, Rev. Lorenzo Albacete, indicated a willingness to meet with us to discuss our programs, help clarify positions, and recommend any adjustments necessary to resolve concerns, but the archbishop would not allow it.

A number of national Catholic organizations issued public statements of support for us as the controversy became more widely known. Our religious congregations received hundreds of letters of personal support for our ministry from individuals it had touched. Several groups volunteered their services in effecting reconciliation. Among them was the General Administrative Team of the Sisters of St. Joseph of Cleveland, who had known and worked with the archbishop personally before he came to Washington. The Sisters' Council of the Archdiocese of Washington

---

urged the archbishop to undertake a process of reconciliation and one of Archbishop Hickey's own Vicars approached him with a similar suggestion. All such proposals for reconciliation were declined.

In May 1984, Bob visited several Roman congregations in the hope that some face to face dialogue at that level might help remedy the situation. But the archbishop had already secured Vatican cooperation. Neither our Provincials nor our Superior Generals were able to effect any kind of due process, despite several attempts.

In July 1984, Cardinal Jerome Hamer, the Prefect of the Congregation for Religious and Secular Institutes, wrote to both Superior Generals and indicated that we must separate ourselves from New Ways Ministry or risk "further disciplinary action." We were instructed not to engage in ministry concerning homosexuality or write on the topic unless we made it clear that "homosexual acts are intrinsically disordered and objectively wrong." We resigned as co-directors from New Ways Ministry in 1984. We continue our educational programs in which we make the magisterial teaching on homogenital behavior quite clear, as we have always done.

Cardinal Hamer communicated the Vatican's decision to the Pro-Nuncio, Pio Laghi, who in turn informed the President of the National Conference of Catholic Bishops, Bishop James Malone. In the fall of 1984 Jeannine moved to Brooklyn, the only diocese on the East coast willing to accept her while she continued her lesbian/gay ministry under the aegis of her congregation. She was affiliated with the Office of Social Action of the Brooklyn Sisters of Mercy until it closed in the summer of 1989. She moved back to the Baltimore archdiocese, where she continues to be assigned to lesbian/gay ministry by the Baltimore Province of the School Sisters of Notre Dame.

In late 1984, Bob was accepted as a chaplain by a Brooklyn

community of De LaSalle Christian Brothers, but was summarily rejected for the position by the Brooklyn Chancellor, Msgr. Otto Garcia, with no explanation or reasons given for the decision. An appeal to Bishop Mugavero proved futile. Bob subsequently relocated to the Archdiocese of Newark, New Jersey, for chaplaincy and pastoral work with faculties from the archdiocese. Two years later, Archbishop Theodore McCarrick, originally an assistant bishop to Cardinal Terence Cooke in the Archdiocese of New York, succeeded Archbishop Peter Gerety, who had taken early retirement. McCarrick refused to renew Bob's faculties when they expired in 1987. Bob later heard that his removal was an item on Bishop McCarrick's agenda even before McCarrick arrived in Newark. In late 1987 Bob relocated to Baltimore while continuing gay-lesbian ministry.

After our departure from Washington, New Ways Ministry sponsored Symposium II, which dealt with gay and lesbian religious and clergy. It was held in 1985-86 in three locations: Washington, D.C., San Francisco, and St. Louis. Each of the gatherings featured prominent Catholic theologians, gay priests and brothers, lesbian sisters, and people who worked in ministry with them. Each drew more than 150 church leaders. In 1985 at the Washington, D.C. event, Archbishop Hickey forbade the celebration of a mass in the hotel and again publicized his opposition to the group to church leadership. We are gratified that the work of New Ways Ministry continues unabated under the able leadership of its board, chaired by Helen Marie Burns, R.S.M., its staff, administrated by Kurt Schade and a pool of faithful volunteers. At this writing, New Ways Ministry is planning for Symposium III in 1992.

As a result of the public controversy surrounding our ministry over the years, and at the request of the Congregation for Religious and Secular Institutes, our religious congregations conducted three studies of our ministry in 1979, in 1981, and in 1985. These included consultations with canon lawyers, moral theologians, participants of our educational programs, and with us. No study found any serious problems with our work or methodology. In 1989, Jeannine's provincial administrator wrote to the United States Catholic Conference and outlined the thorough investigative procedures of the School Sisters of Notre Dame. The letter clearly stated their affirmation of her ministry and requested that such information be communicated to those who raise questions and accusations. In 1986, Bob's provincial wrote to Archbishop Pio Laghi, then pro-nuncio, a supportive letter indicating his belief in the soundness of Bob's presentations based on many positive testimonies.

In 1990, a prominent U. S. archbishop approached Cardinal Hickey to discuss the possibility of a meeting with Hickey or a member of his staff for clarifications. The archbishop indicated that the cardinal's response was very negative. The cardinal's office outlined specific requirements from us prior to any dialogue. These conditions assumed that we are guilty of the initial charge of ambiguity. Naturally, we are less than anxious to undertake a process that presumes guilt, rather than discussing the validity of the charge. It appears that a fair and constructive dialogue with Cardinal Hickey, while desirable from our perspective, seems unlikely in the near future.

Some opposition to our work continues. Mostly it comes from groups such as Catholics United for the Faith, *The Wanderer*, and individuals identified with the pro-life movement. Negative evaluations still come from the Archdiocese of Washington whenever inquiries are made there. It has been our position that the charge of ambiguity is unproven and rather nebulous. We have never been presented with concrete and convincing evidence supporting this accusation. Nor have we been afforded a forum that would provide an unbiased hearing. The charge is periodically resurrected by some church officials whose only source is the judgment provided by the Archdiocese of Washington. Refusals to allow us to speak in Catholic facilities are usually based on ecclesiastical politics or on the fear of perceptions in the local church rather than on issues of doctrine or orthodoxy.

Following the publication of an article by Jeannine on the social discrimination of lesbian women and the church, which appeared in the international theological journal *Concilium,* we learned that the Vatican had received "communications" from European dioceses about it. Naturally we are concerned about the impact on our ministry of such anonymous complaints at such high ecclesiastical levels. This is especially so in a climate in which the Vatican has initiated various official "hearings" for individuals whose work it considers suspect. While an opportunity for an official hearing might prove salutary for us and our work, a great deal would depend on the components of such a process. We were encouraged by the acceptance of "Doctrinal Responsibilities, Approaches to Promoting Cooperation and Resolving Misunderstandings between Bishops and Theologians" by the National Conference of Catholic Bishops in 1989. The third part of this document contains an outline of practical steps for a formal doctrinal dialogue we believe is eminently fair. We continue to seek ways to negotiate carefully the choppy waters of the ecclesiasticalsees.

Since 1984, we have continued to write and speak in a variety of forums in the Catholic community and with a number of organizations, one of which is the Center for Homophobia Education. We are pleased that the Center has chosen to utilize our skills and experiences to conduct seminars in more than 130 of the 169 U.S. dioceses and archdioceses to educate church people about homophobia.

According to one bishop-friend of ours, there are "collegial bishops" and "papal bishops." Since 1984, a number of "collegial bishops" have evaluated our work. They have allowed our programs to take place in Catholic facilities in their dioceses or have sponsored and attended them personally. We are grateful to the many bishops across the country who have taken the time and effort to familiarize themselves with our ministry and to meet with us when we visited their dioceses. Some of them have been kind enough to give us written evaluations of our seminars, all of which have been positive and supportive.

The tensions and conflicts around the topic of homosexuality are affecting all churches and religious groups today. We believe the Catholic community has a great deal of wisdom to bring to a renewed evaluation of societal and religious stances to gay and lesbian persons. Part of our work has been to raise up the gradual development of positive statements, ministries, and analyses in the Catholic community. We realize that the issue of homosexuality is intimately linked to many other areas of ferment in church life such as women, the Christian meaning of sexual pleasure and relationships, celibacy, and the quality of candidates for priesthood.

The HIV-AIDS crisis has added another threatening dimension by relating sexuality to mortality. The church has responded compassionately, though somewhat tardily, to the HIV-AIDS issue and consequently has been confronted with its own teachings, fears, and pastoral responses around homosexuality. We do not see an early resolution to the discussion and debate on homosexuality. Our main hope is that the communal search for truth about human sexuality will be increasingly shaped by reason rather than fear, by compassion rather than condemnation, and by love rather than hate.

Bibliography

Abbott, W. M. (Ed.) (1966). *The documents of Vatican II.* New York: The America Press.

Bailey, D. S. (1975). *Homosexuality and the western Christian tradition.* Hamden, CT: Archon Books.

Baum, G. (1974, February 15). Catholic homosexuals. *Commonweal, 99,* 479-482.

Becker, H. S. (1963). *Outsiders: Studies in the sociology of deviance.* London: Macmillan.

Bell, A., Weinberg, M., & Hammersmith, S. (1981). *Sexual preference: Its development in men and women.* Bloomington, IN: Indiana University Press.

Bieber, I. (1962). *Homosexuality: A psychoanalytic study.* New York: Basic Books.

Blumstein, P. & Schwartz, P. (1983). *American couples.* New York: William Morrow and Co.

Boswell, J. (1980). *Christianity, social tolerance, and homosexuality.* Chicago: University of Chicago Press.

Boswell, J. (1989). Homosexuality and religious life: A historical approach. In J. Gramick (Ed.), *Homosexuality in the priesthood and the religious life.* New York: Crossroad.

Brown, J. (1986). *Immodest acts: The life of a lesbian nun in Renaissance Italy.* New York: Oxford University Press.

Cahill, L. S. (1983). Moral methodology: A case study. In R. Nugent (Ed.), *A challenge to love: Gay and lesbian Catholics in the church.* New York: Crossroad.

Cahill, L. S. (1985a). *Between the sexes: Foundations for a Christian sexual ethics of sexuality.* New York: Paulist Press.

Cahill, L. S. (1985b). Morality: The deepening crisis. *Commonweal,* September, 496-499.

Catholic Council for Church and Society. (1980). *Homosexual people in society.* Mt. Rainier, MD: New Ways Ministry.

Catholic Social Welfare Commission. (1981). *An introduction to the pastoral care of homosexual people.* Mt. Rainier, MD: New Ways Ministry.

Chandler, R. (1987). The Times Poll: Americans like pope but challenge doctrine. *Los Angeles Times,* August 23, 1, 20.

Chang, J. & Block, J. (1960). A study of identification in male homosexuals, *Journal of Consulting Psychology, 24,* 307-310.

Churchill, W. (1967). *Homosexual behavior among males.* Englewood Cliffs, NJ: Prentice-Hall.

Coccioli, C. (1966). *Fabrizio's book.* New York: Shorecrest.

Coleman, G. D. (1984). The homosexual question in the priesthood and religious life. *The Priest,* December, 12-19.

Commission for the Plan of Pastoral Action for Family Ministry. (1979, Sept. 22). *Responding to the call.* Milwaukee: Archdiocese of Milwaukee.

Congregation for the Doctrine of the Faith. (1976). *Declaration on certain questions concerning sexual ethics.* Washington, DC: United States Catholic Conference.

Congregation for the Doctrine of the Faith. (1986). Letter to the Bishops of the Catholic Church on the pastoral care of homosexual persons. In J. Gramick and R. Nugent (Eds.), *The Vatican and homosexuality.* New York: Crossroad, 1988.

Curb, R. & Manahan, N. (Eds.). (1985). *Lesbian nuns: Breaking silence.* Tallahassee, FL: Naiad Press.

Curran, C. (1983). Moral theology and homosexuality. In J. Gramick (Ed.), *Homosexuality and the Catholic church.* Chicago: Thomas More Press.

Eisler, B. (1991). *O'Keeffe and Stieglitz: An American romance.* New York: Bantam.

Farley, M. (1983). An ethic for same-sex relations. In R. Nugent (Ed.), *A challenge to love: Gay and lesbian Catholics in the church.* New York: Crossroad.

Ford, C.S. & Beach, F.A. (1951). *Patterns of sexual behavior.* New York: Harper Colophon.

Fortunato, J. E. (1982). *Embracing the exile: Healing journeys of gay Christians.* New York: Seabury Press.

Francoeur, R. T. (1991). *Becoming a sexual person* (2nd ed.) New York: Macmillan.

Gagnon, J. H. & Simon, W. S. (1968). Sexual deviance in contemporary America. *Annals of the American Academy of Political and Social Science,* 376, 107-122.

Gallagher, J. (Ed.). (1986). *Homosexuality and the magisterium.* Mt. Rainier, MD: New Ways Ministry.

Gallagher, R. (1979, September). Understanding the homosexual. *The Furrow,* 555-569.

Gallup, G., Jr. & Castelli, J. (1987). *The American people: Their beliefs, practices, and values.* Garden City, NY: Doubleday.

Gebhard, P. H., Gagnon, J. H., Pomeroy, W. B. & Christensen, C. V. (1965). *Sex offenders: An analysis of types.* New York: Harper & Row.

Gittings, B. (1969). The homosexual and the church. In R. W. Weltge (Ed.), *The same sex.* Philadelphia: Pilgrim Press.

Glaser, C. (1990). *Come home! Reclaiming spirituality and community as gay men and lesbians.* San Francisco: Harper & Row.

Gorer, G. (1964). *The American people,* rev. ed. New York: Norton.

Gramick, J. (Ed.). (1983). *Homosexuality and the Catholic church.* Chicago: Thomas More Press.

Gramick, J. (1988). Rome speaks, the church responds. In J. Gramick & R. Nugent (Eds.), *The Vatican and homosexuality.* New York: Crossroad.

Gramick, J. (Ed.) (1989) *Homosexuality in the priesthood and the religious life.* New York: Crossroad.

Gramick, J. & Nugent, R. (1979). Open book: Review of Masters and Johnson's Homosexuality in perspective. *Insight*, 3, 4, 12-13.

Gramick, J. & Nugent, R. (Ed.). (1988). *The Vatican and homosexuality.* New York: Crossroad.

Grippo, D. (1990, September). Why lesbian and gay Catholics stay Catholic. *U.S. Catholic*, 55, 9, 18-25.

Guindon, A. (1977). *The sexual language.* Ottawa: The University of Ottawa Press.

Guindon, A. (1986). *The sexual creators: An ethical proposal for concerned Christians.* Lanham, MD: University of America Press.

Guindon, A. (1988). Homosexual acts or gay speech. In J. Gramick & R. Nugent (Eds.), *The Vatican and homosexuality.* New York: Crossroad.

Hanigan, J. P. (1988). *Homosexuality: The test case for Christian sexual ethics.* New York: Paulist Press.

Harris, B. (1978). Lesbians in literature: An introduction. In G. Vida (Ed.), *Our right to love.* Englewood Cliffs, NJ: Prentice-Hall.

Harvey, J. F. (1987). *The homosexual person: New thinking in pastoral care.* San Francisco: St. Ignatius Press.

Helldorfer, M. (1982). Homosexual brothers: Sources of new life. In T. McCarthy (Ed.), *Prejudice.* Romeoville, IL: Christian Brothers National Office.

Hellwig, M. (1987). *The role of the theologian.* Kansas City, MO: Sheed and Ward.

Heyward, C. I. (1982). *The redemption of God: A theology of mutual relation.* New York: University Press of America.

Heyward, C. I. (1987, Spring). Heterosexist theology: Being above it all. *Journal of Feminist Studies in Religion*, 3, 1, 29-38.

Heyward, C. (1989). *Touching our strength: The erotic as power and the love of God.* San Francisco: Harper & Row.

Hock, P. & Zubin, J. (1949). *Psychosexual development in health and disease.* New York: Grune and Stratton.

Hoffman, M. (1969). *The gay world.* New York: Bantam Books.

Hooker, E. (1957). The adjustment of the male overt homosexual. *Journal of Projective Techniques*, 21, 18-31.

Irish Hierarchy. (1985). *Love is for life.* Dublin: Veritas Publications.

John Paul II. (1981, Dec. 24). The apostolic exhortation on the family. *Origins*, 11 (28 & 29), 437-468.

Jones, M. K. (1966). *Toward a Christian understanding of the homosexual.* New York: Association Press.

Jung, C. G. (1959). *The collected works*, trans. R. F. C. Hull. New York: Pantheon.

Kallmann, F. J. (1952a). Comparative twin study on the genetic aspects of male homosexuality. *Journal of Nervous and Mental Disease*, 115, 4, 283-298.

Kallmann, F. J. (1952b). Twin and sibship study of overt male homosexuality. *American Journal of Human Genetics*, 4, 2, 136-146.

Keane, P. (1977). *Sexual morality: A Catholic perspective*. New York: Paulist Press.

Kelsey, D. (1984). Homosexuality and the church: Theological issues. *Reflection*, 80, 3, 9-12.

Kinsey, A. C., Pomeroy, W. B. & Martin, C. E. (1948). *Sexual behavior in the human male*. Philadelphia: Saunders.

Kinsey, A. C., Pomeroy, W. B., Martin, C. E. & Gebhard, P. H. (1953). *Sexual behavior in the human female*. Philadelphia: Saunders.

Klaich, D. (1974). *Woman plus woman: Attitudes toward lesbianism*. New York: Simon and Schuster.

Klintworth, G. K. (1962). A pair of male monozygotic twins discordant for homosexuality. *Journal of Nervous and Mental Disease*, 135, 2, 113-125.

Kosnik, A., Carroll, W., Cunningham, A., Modras, R., & Schulte, J. (1977). *Human sexuality: New directions in American Catholic thought*. New York: Paulist Press.

LeVay, S. (1991, August 30). A difference in hypothalamic structure between heterosexual and homosexual men. *Science*, 253, 1034-1037.

Levinson, D. (1978). *The seasons of a man's life*. New York: Ballantine Books.

Maguire, D. (1983). The morality of homosexual marriage. In R. Nugent (Ed.), *A challenge to love: Gay and lesbian Catholics in the church*. New York: Crossroad.

Malloy, E. (1981). *Homosexuality and the Christian way of life*. Washington, D.C.: University Press of America.

Marcus, R. (1990, October 26). Powell regrets backing sodomy laws. *The Washington Post*.

Masters, W. H. & Johnson, V. E. (1979). *Homosexuality in perspective*. Boston: Little, Brown, and Company.

McCormick, R. (1989). *The critical calling: Reflections on moral dilemmas since Vatican II*. Washington, DC: Georgetown University Press.

McNaught, B. (1988). *On being gay: Thoughts on family, faith, and love*. New York: St. Martin's Press.

McNeill, J. (1976). *The church and the homosexual*. Kansas City: Sheed, Andrews and McMeel.

McNeill, J. (1988). *Taking a chance on God: Liberating theology for gays, lesbians, and their lovers, families, and friends*. Boston: Beacon Press.

Money, J. (1986). *Lovemaps: Clinical concepts of sexual/erotic health and pathology, paraphilia, and gender transposition in childhood, adolescence, and maturity*. New York: Irvington Publishers.

Moran, G. (1977). Sexual forms. In *Sexuality and brotherhood*. Lockport, IL: Christian Brothers Conference.

Murphy, S. (1983). *Midlife wanderer: The woman religious in midlife transition*. Whitinsville, MA: Affirmation Books.

Murphy, S. (1986, Winter). Counseling lesbian women religious. *Women and Therapy*, 5, 4, 7-17.

National Conference of Catholic Bishops. (1976). *To live in Christ Jesus*. Washington, D.C.: United States Catholic Conference.

National Conference of Religious Vocation Directors. (1986, May). *NCRVD special report*. Chicago: National Conference of Religious Vocation Directors.

New Zealand Catholic Bishops' Conference. (1986, October 19). Dignity, love, life: Statement on homosexuality. *Zealandia*, 52, 42, 10, 19.

Nugent, R. (1981). Homosexuality and the hurting family. *America*, 144, 154-157.

Nugent, R. (Ed.). (1983). *A challenge to love: Gay and lesbian Catholics in the church*. New York: Crossroad.

Nugent, R. (1988). Sexual orientation in Vatican thinking. In J. Gramick & R. Nugent, *The Vatican and homosexuality*. New York: Crossroad.

Nugent, R. (1989). *Prayer journey for persons with AIDS*. Cincinnati, OH: St. Anthony Messenger Press.

Nugent, R. & Gramick, J. (Eds.). (1982). *A time to speak*. Mt. Rainier, MD: New Ways Ministry.

Pare, C. M. B. (1956). Homosexuality and chromosomal sex, *Journal of Psychosomatic Research*, 1, 4, 247-251.

Pearson, C. L. (1986). *Good-bye, I love you*. New York: Jove Books.

Plummer, K. (1975). *Sexual stigma: An interactionist account*. London: Routledge & Kegan Paul.

Pomeroy, W. B. (1969). Homosexuality. In R. W. Weltge (Ed.), *The same sex*. Philadelphia: Pilgrim Press.

Richards, D. (1990). *Lesbian lists: A look at lesbian culture, history, and personalities*. Boston: Alyson Publications.

Rossetti, S. J. (Ed.). (1990). *Slayer of the soul: Child sexual abuse and the Catholic Church*. Mystic, CT: Twenty-Third Publications.

Rowse, A. L. (1977). *Homosexuals in history: A study of ambivalence in society, literature and the arts*. New York: Macmillan.

Ruether, R. (1989). Homophobia, heterosexism, and pastoral practice. In J. Gramick (Ed.), *Homosexuality in the priesthood and in the religious life*. New York: Crossroad.

Senate of Priests. (1983). *Ministry and homosexuality in the archdiocese of San Francisco*. San Francisco: Senate of Priests.

Seubert, X. J. (1991). The sacramentality of metaphors: Reflections on homosexuality. *Cross Currents*, 41, 1, 52-68.

Sipe, A. W. R. (1990). *A secret world: Sexuality and the search for celibacy*. New York: Brunner/Mazel.

Sipe, A. W. R. (1991, May 18). Education for celibacy: An American challenge. *America*, 164, 19, 539-540, 547-548.

Sister Mary. (1989). The lost coin. In J. Gramick (Ed.), *Homosexuality in the priesthood and the religious life*. New York: Crossroad.

Teichner, S. (1989, June 5). Results of poll. *San Francisco Examiner*, 13.

Thomas, P. (1983). Gay and lesbian ministry during marital breakdown and the annulment process. In R. Nugent (Ed.), *A challenge to love: Gay and lesbian Catholics in the church*. New York: Crossroad.

Thompson, Jr., N. L., McCandless, B. R., & Strickland, B. R. (1971). Personal adjustment of male and female homosexuals and heterosexuals. *Journal of Abnormal Psychology, 78*, 237-240.

Tobin, K. & Wicker, R. (1972). *The gay crusaders*. New York: Paperback Library.

Tri-Conference Retirement Office. (1990, April). *Retirement needs survey of United States religious-III*. Washington, DC: United States Catholic Conference.

United States Catholic Conference. (1981). *Planning for single young adult ministry: Directions for ministerial outreach*. Washington, DC: United States Catholic Conference.

Washington State Catholic Conference. (1983, April 28). *The prejudice against homosexuals and the ministry of the church*. Seattle: Washington State Catholic Conference.

Weakland, R. (1980, July 18). Who is my neighbor? *The Milwaukee Herald Citizen*.

Weinberg, M. S. & Williams, C. J. (1974). *Male homosexuals*. New York: Oxford University Press.

Wolf, J. (Ed.). (1989). *Gay priests*. San Francisco: Harper & Row.

Woods, R. (1977). *Another kind of love: Homosexuality and spirituality*. Chicago: Thomas More Press.

Young, L. (1971, August 23). Militant homosexual; Gay liberation movement. *Newsweek, 78*, 45-48.

Zanotti, B. (Ed.). (1986). *A faith of one's own: Explorations by Catholic lesbians*. Trumansburg, NY: The Crossing Press.

Index

Resources

Archdiocesan Catholic
  Gay and Lesbian Ministry
Archdiocese of Seattle
910 Marion St.
Seattle, WA 98104

Archdiocesan Gay and Lesbian
  Outreach (AGLO)
Archdiocese of Baltimore
320 Cathedral St.
Baltimore, MD 21201

Archdiocese of Milwaukee
Cousins Catholic Center
3501 S. Lake Dr.
Box 07912
Milwaukee, WI 53207

Board of Ministry to Homosexual
  Men and Women
Archdiocese of San Francisco
441 Church St.
San Francisco, CA 94114

Catholic Advocates for Lesbian
  and Gay Rights
834 W. Agatite
Chicago, IL 60640

Committee on Sexual Minorities
Diocese of Richmond
811 Cathedral Place
Richmond, VA 23220

Conference for Catholic Lesbians
Box 436
Planetarium Station
New York, NY 10024

Diocese of Dallas
Family Life Office
3915 Lemmon Ave.
Box 190507
Dallas, TX 75219

Ministry to Homosexual Catholics
Archdiocese of Washington
Social Services
5001 Eastern Ave.
Washington, DC 20017

Outreach Services for Gay
  and Lesbian Persons & Families
Diocese of Oakland
433 Jefferson St.
Oakland, CA 94607

Stepping Stones
Diocese of Charlotte
Box 36776
Charlotte, NC 28236

Archdiocesan Gay
  and Lesbian Outreach/AGLO
Archdiocese of Chicago
155 E. Superior St.
Chicago, IL 60611

Archdiocese of Los Angeles
Pastoral Ministry to Gay
  and Lesbian Ministry
1281 N. Fairfax Ave.
Los Angeles, CA 90046

Bishop's Representative
Diocese of Erie
205 W. 9th St.
Erie, PA 16501

Caritas
Diocese of Camden
Family Life Office
1845 Haddon Ave.
Camden, NJ 08101

Catholic Pastoral Committee
  on Sexual Minorities
Box 581391
Minneapolis, MN 55458-1391

Committee for Pastoral Care
  with and to Gay and Lesbian Persons
Diocese of Buffalo
170 Kerns Avenue
Buffalo, NY 14211

Dignity, Inc.
1500 Massachusetts Ave., NW
Suite 11
Washington, DC 20005

Diocese of Kansas City-St. Joseph
Catholic Charities
Box 419037
Kansas City, MO 64141

New Ways Ministry
4012 29th St.
Mt. Rainier, MD 20712

Pastoral Resource Committee
Diocese of San Jose
841 Lenzen Ave.
San Jose, CA 95126

Christian Community Association
Box 693
Madison, WI 53701-0693

Communication Ministry, Inc.
Box 60125
Chicago, IL 60660